London's Water Wars
The Competition for London's Water Supply in the Nineteenth Century

John Graham-Leigh joined the
Metropolitan Water Board in 1970 and
subsequently worked for its successor
Thames Water until 2000, when he
retired to pursue his historical
researches. From 1993 to 2000 he was
Thames Water's Regulation and Policy
Manager. He is married with two children
and lives in Barnet, Hertfordshire.

John Graham-Leigh

London's Water Wars

The Competition for London's
Water Supply in the
Nineteenth Century

Francis
Boutle
Publishers

First published by Francis Boutle Publishers
23 Arlington Way
London EC1R 1UY
Tel/Fax: (020) 7278 4497
Email:waterwars@francisboutle.demon.co.uk
www.francisboutle.demon.co.uk

ISBN 1 903427 02 9

Printed in Great Britain by Redwood Books

Acknowledgements

Most of this book was written between 1982 and 1984 as an Open University master's thesis about the competition in 1810–1817 over London's water supply; also included is an earlier essay on the Metropolis Water Act 1852 which to some extent continues the story.

When I finished the thesis in 1984 the politics of London's water supply appeared to have been settled firmly in favour of public ownership and control – competition was not even thought of. Water was such an obvious monopoly, with such enormous capital start-up costs and such a need for long-term planning, that there was no debate on the subject. Now, only sixteen years later, water supply is once again in private hands and competition is accepted as something which will inevitably arrive in the near future – indeed, is already here as far as the largest customers are concerned. Aggressive new companies are emerging, seeking a share of what are seen as unwarrantably high profits enjoyed by the incumbents.

The situation is almost back where it was nearly two centuries ago. How has this happened? Have the lessons of the ruinous competition of 1810–1817 been completely forgotten? I have addressed this in Chapter 9, which is entirely new. Chapters 1 to 7, which constitute the greater part of the original thesis, have been revised only to the extent of minor updating and correcting.

My thanks are due firstly to the Thames Water Authority, which allowed me to study the archives on which this thesis is based, together with its fine collection of books and Parliamentary Papers concerning London's water supply. Its successor, Thames Water Utilities, kindly provided many of the illustrations. Other institutions which permitted me to use their facilities included the British Library, the Institute of Historical Research at the University of London, the Guildhall Library, the National Register of Archives, the Public Record Office, the House of Lords Record Office and the Institution of Civil Engineers. I would like to express my gratitude to them. Individuals who have given me their help and encouragement include Professor Theo Barker of the London School of

Economics, Dr Francis Sheppard, late of the Greater London Council, and Ian Donnachie of the Open University. Colin Millikin of Thames Water encouraged me to seek publication, for which I am grateful, Julian Putkowski made the author's task easy through the publication process, and numerous colleagues at Thames Water who gave advice. To all of them my thanks. Finally, my wife's services as critic and proof-reader have been invaluable.

Contents

List of illustrations

Chapter 1
The possessors: the old water companies to 1805

At the start of the nineteenth century London north of the Thames was supplied with water by a number of long-established companies. The oldest was the London Bridge Water Works, established by Peter Morris, a German or Dutchman, in 1581. In that year Morris was granted a 500-year lease of the first arch at the northern end of London Bridge, in which he erected a water-wheel to raise Thames water for distribution through the southern and eastern parts of the city by means of wooden pipes. The water works itself was destroyed in the Great Fire of 1666 but re-erected shortly after, and by the mid-eighteenth century had five water-wheels occupying three arches of the bridge. In 1761 an additional wheel was erected in order to extend the supply to Southwark.[1] In 1809 the works supplied an average of nearly four million gallons of water per day to some 10,000 consumers, and had a gross income from water rents of about £12,000 per annum.[2] The average charge per house had scarcely altered for a century, remaining at about 20s. per annum.[3] Although charges were reasonable for the volume of water supplied, the works' powers of supply were limited by the height to which water could be raised by the water-wheels, and many consumers, therefore, preferred to take the New River Company's water. The London Bridge works had no space to erect a steam engine, so could not provide a 'high service' or supply of water to the upper storeys of houses.

The Morris family sold the works in 1701 to Richard Soame, who also extended the area of supply by acquiring a lease of certain public conduits from the City Corporation. Soame's undertaking had a nominal capital of £150,000, ini-

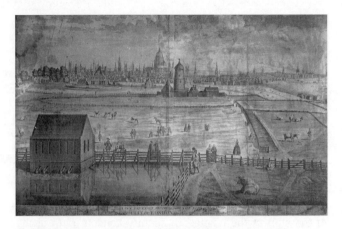

The New River Head, 1729. The 'Upper Pond' (now Claremont Square Reservoir) is in the foreground.

tially in three hundred £500 shares, and by 1708 the capital had been divided into 1,500 £100 shares. At the end of the eighteenth century the London Bridge works was moderately profitable; dividends of 2% on the nominal capital were paid annually from 1794 to 1797, and of 3% from 1798 to 1811. The nominal £100 shares changed hands for only £70 apiece between 1789 and 1811, however, so that purchasers enjoyed a higher rate of return on their investment.[4]

The New River Company was a much bigger and better known enterprise. It originated soon after the London Bridge concern, with Acts of Parliament obtained by the City Corporation in 1606 and 1607 empowering the undertakers of the scheme to bring water from springs at Chadwell and Amwell, near Hertford, by means of a conduit or tunnel. The Corporation granted powers to Hugh Myddelton, a London goldsmith, in 1609, and he and 28 other 'Adventurers' each subscribed £500 towards the cost of constructing a conduit. The New River was built over a distance of 40 miles from Amwell to Clerkenwell between 1609 and 1613, and the 'Company of the New River brought from Chadwell and Amwell to London' was incorporated by Royal Charter in 1619. By 1636 the company's capital was divided into 72 shares, of which 36 were known as Adventurers' Shares and the other 36 as King's Shares.[5] Most of the King's Shares, and also a few of the Adventurers' Shares, carried with them an obligation to pay a charge averaging £13.17s.9½d. per share per annum to the Crown; this was known as the 'Crown Clogg' and resulted from the partial financing by King James I of the original construction of the New River.[6]

The water carried in the New River discharged into a pond at New River Head, Clerkenwell, at a height of some 84 feet above the level of the Thames, and from where it was distributed by gravity through a system of wooden pipes to consumers in various parts of the city. About 1709 the company constructed an 'Upper Pond' at a higher level immediately to the north of New River Head so that houses on higher ground could also be served; water was raised to this pond initially by a windmill and later by a horse-mill. Soon after the company began operations increasing demand rendered the quantity of water obtainable from the Chadwell and Amwell springs insufficient, and from 1660 the supply was supplemented by water drawn from the River Lee near Hertford.[7] In 1809 the company served some 59,000 houses in the City, the areas between there and Westminster, and outlying districts to the north and east. An average of about 11 million gallons of water a day was supplied in return for a gross rental of £81,000, an average of about 27s. 6d. per house per annum.[8]

In its early years the New River Company had shown only small profits, but by the late eighteenth century the proprietors were receiving considerable annual dividends. The value of the shares is hard to determine, but in 1815 the Company estimated its capital at £750,000, giving a notional value of over £10,000 for each of the 72 shares.[9] The 36 Adventurers' Shares were more valuable than the King's Shares, which were generally burdened with the Crown Clogg and did not give their owners the right to serve as directors. Annual dividends between 1789 and 1810 varied between £396 and £486 per share; by that time some of the shares were divided among part-owners into as many as 32 parts, but 27 King's Shares and 30 Adventurers' Shares were still complete.[10]

The third largest company in terms of water supplied was the Chelsea Water Works Company, incorporated by letters patent in 1723 to supply the City of Westminster and adjacent places, and with an original capital of £40,000 in 2,000 £20 shares. The company ran into financial difficulties while its works were being constructed, and in 1733 it was necessary to raise further capital. No investors could be found to take new £20 shares, however, so 2,000 £10 shares were issued, the proprietors of these having the same voting and dividend rights as the holders of the original issue. The Chelsea Company initially raised water from the Thames at Chelsea by water-wheels and horse-mills, discharged it into two reservoirs at Green Park and one in Walnut Tree Walk, Hyde Park, and then piped it to consumers through wooden mains.[11] In 1809 the company supplied 9,500 houses in Westminster and Chelsea with about 1¼ million gallons per day. Its gross rental in that year was nearly £15,000, the average annual charge of over 30s per house reflecting the better class of the houses in its area of supply.[12] In its early years the company was not profitable (no dividends at all were declared before 1737 or between 1740 and 1753), but by 1797 the proprietors were dividing profits of £2,000 per annum, representing a rate of just over 3% on the £60,000 nominal capital.[13] The company was also able to accumulate a reserve in Consols, amounting to £40,000 in 1810, against possible extraordinary expenditures.[14] During the early years of the nineteenth century the company was extending its area of supply northwards through Marylebone up to and beyond the New Road (now Marylebone Road).[15]

The York Buildings Company (The Governor and Company of Undertakers for raising the Thames Water in York Buildings) was incorporated by Act of Parliament in 1691 and its works occupied a site near the Strand at Charing Cross. Initially water was raised to an elevated cistern by a horse-mill and distributed in wooden pipes to consumers in the surrounding parts of Westminster – also a well-to-do area.[16] The company's capital totalled £21,000 in 84 £250 shares, and its rental in 1810 amounted to £3,400 from 2,250 consumers, who thus paid an average of about 30s. each per annum. The amount of water supplied averaged 150,000 gallons per day.[17] The company went through many vicissitudes in the eighteenth century; after the 1715 Jacobite rising it invested heavily in buying confiscated land, and in the 'Bubble' of 1720 its shares rose to enormous prices before collapsing. In 1732–35 its affairs were the subject of a Parliamentary inquiry, which found it to be losing £10,000 a year, and by 1792 all its property other than the water works had been sold to pay creditors.[18] At the end of the eighteenth century profits were meagre; the proprietors received no dividends between 1795 and 1800, then an £8 per share dividend in 1801, nothing in 1802 or 1803, £4 per share in 1804, then nothing until 1810.[19]

Between them the London Bridge, New River, Chelsea and York Buildings Water Works supplied all the piped water in London north of the Thames before 1806. Three other water companies supplied outlying areas soon to become part of the expanding metropolis. The Hampstead Water Company, incorporated in 1692, supplied water to the villages of Hampstead and Highgate from ponds on Hampstead Heath, but was a very small concern.[20] Considerably larger was the Shadwell Water Works, which began operations in 1669 and was incorporated in 1692. Until 1750 the works consisted of a horse-mill which raised water for distribution to consumers in Shadwell, Stepney and Wapping. The company was bought by the London Dock Company in 1801 for £50,000.[21] In 1808 the Shadwell works supplied about '8,000 houses besides Sugar houses and breweries which is equal to the full extent of its power so that any additional supply from it at present is altogether out of the Question'.[22] The third company was the West Ham Water Works, which commenced in 1743 (incorporated 1747). This raised water from the River Lee at Bow and supplied consumers in Mile End and Stratford. The West Ham and Shadwell companies competed against each other until 1785, when they agreed a boundary giving each an exclusive area of supply, and in 1800–1801 were both bought by the London Dock Company which continued their operation without seeking to improve their efficiency. In 1808 the West Ham works supplied about 2,250 houses and were estimated to be capable of supplying up to 2,000 more.[23] The two companies between them had a rental of £10,000 in 1809, an average of less than 20s. per house, demonstrating that the areas they supplied were generally poorer than those further west. With an average daily supply of approximately 600,000 gallons, they also supplied less water per house than any of the London companies with the exception of the York Buildings.[24]

The total amount of water supplied by the 'old' companies in 1809 (excluding the Hampstead Company, for which no figures are available) was on average about 17 million gallons per day. No doubt a considerable proportion of the total was taken by large consumers who used water for trade purposes,

Wooden water pipe. A typical section of wooden 'service'. The hole for the customer's 'communication pipe' is apparent.

but it is not possible to give any figures as the companies did not keep such records.[25] The total number of 'houses' (including trade premises) supplied was 92,000, so each house theoretically received, on average, 185 gallons of water each day.[26] This implies an average allowance of some 23 gallons per day for each person supplied, using the accepted average of eight people per house. This is a surprisingly large amount – in 1984 the Thames Water Authority estimated that each of its eleven million consumers used 35 gallons per day for domestic purposes. We may assume the amount actually received by consumers in the early nineteenth century was considerably less than 23 gallons per day, however.

The Romans had used lead pipes for distributing water, but in sixteenth century London, when piped supplies were re-introduced on a large scale for the first time in over a millennium, it was found cheaper to use wooden pipes for all but the smallest sizes.[27] For the next two centuries the standard distribution system remained a series of wooden pipes, usually of 7-inch bore, leading from the company's reservoir or water tower to a network of smaller wooden pipes through the

streets to be served. Small lead 'communication pipes' were
inserted into the wooden 'services' and led into the consumers' premises.

This system of distribution was defective in several
respects. The entire system was gravity fed, so that only those
consumers living at a much lower level than that of the reservoir would have had a supply at a reasonable pressure. Since
the level of the reservoir at New River Head was only 84 feet
above the level of the Thames, for instance, many of the New
River Company's consumers must have received a trickle
rather than a flow of water.[28] No improvement in the pressure
was practicable so long as wooden pipes were used, because
these would not withstand a pumped, high-pressure supply.
Even with the traditional low-pressure gravity feed, the wood-
en pipes were far from perfect. Generally made out of elm
trunks, they were bored by long augers driven by water- or
horse-mills (the New River Company had a pipe-boring yard
with a horse-mill at Dorset Stairs in the City), and were jointed
by ramming the tapered top of the pipe into the countersunk
butt of the next pipe; the butt was generally reinforced by an
iron hoop to avoid splitting.[29] The standard length of each elm
pipe was nine feet. The maximum bore of pipes made out of
elm trunks was 12-inch, and 7-inch was the largest common-
ly in use.[30] This restriction in the size of pipes meant that several parallel lines of pipes had to be used to convey the main
supply of water from the reservoir, such lines of pipes being
called 'mains' to distinguish them from the single 'services'. In
1756 the London Bridge Water Works had eight 7-inch pipes
leading from the water tower to the distribution network, the
York Buildings Company had two, the Chelsea Company had
five pipes (one 8-inch, three 7-inch, one 6-inch). The New
River Company had the massive total of fifty-eight 7-inch
pipes to convey the water of the New River into the City,[31] and
in 1810 its largest main, leading down Goswell Street (now
Goswell Road), consisted of nine parallel 7-inch pipes.[32]

Leakages from wooden pipes were very frequent; the thin-
ner wood of the butt and taper of a joint provided a weak point
so that a relatively short period of rotting would allow water to
leak out. The system of rows of pipes in the same street made
locating the source of any leakage very difficult, and streets
were constantly being excavated in the course of searching for
and remedying leakages.[33] In 1810 a Commissioner of Paving

for the parish of St James, for example, gave evidence before a parliamentary committee of 'the great destruction of the pavement by taking up the pipes, which is a very great annoyance', and, before the same committee, Counsel for the West Middlesex Water Works Company said that 'with the Chelsea pipes all over the district, there are as many springs as if it were a place for woodcocks and snipes', giving rise to 'a sort of marshy ground, where springs rise up round Coventry-street'.[34] Also in 1810, the Engineer of the East London Water Works Company reported that 'Where the streets are worst is occasioned by leakage from the New River pipes, the water being on at the time ... we could ascertain that fact by seeing where the water rose, in a great many places washing up the soil, and occasioning the Pavement to fall'.[35] In 1821 the Engineer of the New River Company estimated that a quarter of the whole amount of water raised had been lost through leaks from wooden pipes,[36] and this was almost certainly an underestimate.

The procedure by which water was actually delivered to consumers' houses caused further wastage. There were normally no individual stopcocks on communication pipes, and on 'water day' (which normally came round three times a week) the company's turncock would open a valve controlling the wooden service pipe in the street. Water then filled the service from the main and automatically entered each communication pipe, which terminated in a cistern or water butt in the consumer's basement. The turncock left the valve open for a period long enough to allow the cisterns to fill, about two hours. Any cisterns which had already been partly full, or were of inadequate size, overflowed unless they were fitted with ballcocks, which were then uncommon. Once the controlling valve was shut, the service would empty through the communication pipes until only a small amount remained in the bottom of the pipe. The services were not kept full of water, and even the mains were generally left empty at night.

While distribution systems remained unimproved until the beginning of the nineteenth century, some technical improvements had been made in the capital equipment of water works during the eighteenth century. Horse and water power were gradually displaced by the steam engine for pumping to reservoirs and water towers. The first London water company to erect a steam engine was the York Buildings Company, which in 1712 installed an atmospheric engine, of the type recently invented by Thomas Savery, for 'raising water by fire' from the Thames to its water tower. This engine was soon abandoned as its high consumption of coal made it uneconomic, but in 1726 the Company installed another atmospheric engine, of the improved type designed by Newcomen. This engine was used for five years before it was decided that it also consumed too much coal and was abandoned.[37] The continuous history of steam pumping in London begins with the installation of two Newcomen engines at the Chelsea Company's works in 1741 and 1742.[38] They were a great success as replacements for the old water-mill, and the Chelsea Company's example was soon followed by others. The Shadwell Water Works replaced its horse-mill by two steam engines in 1750, and in 1752 the York Buildings Company erected a third atmospheric engine, this time as a permanent installation.[39] In 1766 the New River Company installed an atmospheric engine of the Newcomen type, as improved by John Smeaton, to raise water to a tower at New River Head, enabling the Company to supply houses on higher ground.[40] After James Watt had patented his separate condenser engine in 1769 and begun his partnership with Matthew Boulton in 1775, steam engines of this more efficient type were soon introduced by the London water companies. The first of the Boulton and Watt engines was erected at Shadwell in 1778, and was followed by others at Chelsea (1778) and New River Head (replacing Smeaton's engine, 1786).[41] By 1800, therefore, most of the companies relied wholly or mainly on steam pumping to raise water to their reservoirs. Water-wheels and horse-mills remained in use, however, and there was still no pumping into the distribution systems.

The other great improvement introduced during the eighteenth century was much less widespread. This was the cast iron water pipe, first used by the Chelsea Company in about 1746.[42] It lasted longer than the wooden pipe, which had a maximum useful life of twenty-five years and was generally expected to last for an average of fourteen years. In some soils, wooden pipes could require replacement after only four years.[43] For most of the eighteenth century, however, the high cost of iron and difficulty in obtaining a watertight joint precluded the introduction of iron pipes on a large scale. Until

1785 iron pipes were generally flanged at both ends and were jointed by bolting the flanges together. This method did not always produce a satisfactory joint, and in 1785 Thomas Simpson, Engineer of the Chelsea Company, introduced the 'spigot and socket' joint, which could be stuffed tight with tow and sealed with lead.[44] This technique was extensively used in later years, but the continued high cost of iron meant that at the beginning of the nineteenth century it was used only in especially important situations where pumping was necessary, such as the rising mains at London Bridge (vertical pipes carrying water from the wheels to the elevated reservoir) and the main pipes from the Thames to the reservoirs at Chelsea.[45] The distribution systems continued to be entirely of wood.

The unsatisfactory nature of the companies' supplies naturally led to numerous complaints from consumers. Although Thomas Simpson testified before a parliamentary committee in 1810 that, as Engineer of the Chelsea Company, he 'never had any complaints, either of the badness of the water or of insufficient supply', the same committee heard much evidence to the contrary, principally from Fire Offices. The mains and services, of course, were not kept full at night (Simpson testifying that if the mains were kept full, wastage of water through leakage would increase and dishonest turncocks would supply their friends with water free of charge), and the utility of the wooden 'fire plugs' which the companies provided on their pipes was, therefore, limited.[46] The plugs were supposed to be drawn only by the companies' turncocks, and in the event of a fire occurring at night application had to be made to the appropriate company's works (in most instances New River Head) for the main to be filled, before water could be obtained for fire-fighting.[47] This sometimes led to a delay of several hours before a fire could be fought effectively, and the Fire Offices were very dissatisfied with the system. William Yambold, for example, a former parish officer giving evidence in 1810, instanced a fire in Frith Street, Soho, in 1804 or 1805 when he had applied to the turncock for water but none had been available because the turncock, 'a stupid Irishman, as most of them are', had not complied promptly enough. Much additional damage had, therefore, been caused. As a result of this incident a well had been dug in Soho Square to provide water for fire-fighting.[48] Irregularity in supply also caused great annoyance. A member of the St George's Paving

Committee, George Halfhide of Coventry Street, complained that he was 'sometimes ten days without water', Richard Thomas of High Holborn testified that 'we are very often out of water, for a week or more together', and Henry Barnes of Princes Street had tried bribing the turncock and complaining to the General Committee of the New River Company, without obtaining any regularity in supply. The 1810 Committee heard these and other similar complaints.[49]

Water quality does not seem to have been considered so important; the discovery that water pollution and disease were connected lay half a century in the future, and water which was not obviously discoloured or malodorous was regarded as satisfactory. Even foul water was not necessarily viewed with concern: Ralph Dodd, the engineer and water company promoter, wrote in 1805 that 'Thames water being kept in wooden vessels, after a few months, often becomes apparently putrid ... and produces a disagreeable smell. But even when drunk in this state, it never produces sickness; therefore it is evident no harm or ill occurs to persons whose resolution, notwithstanding its offensive smell, induces them to drink it'.[50] James Pitt of Coventry Street testified in 1810 that the Chelsea Company's water was 'thicker' than and 'considerable inferior' to the New River Company's but the number of complaints of 'bad water' was far outnumbered by complaints of insufficient supply.[51]

The water companies normally undertook to turn on the water in each street service on alternate days, other than Sundays, that is three times per week. Demand was outstripping the companies' ability to supply, and defects in their distribution systems added further difficulties. London was growing rapidly in size and population: in 1776 it contained some 700,000 people, but by 1801 there were 957,000.[52] The fastest growth was in newly built-up areas such as St Pancras, whose population increased from around 600 in 1770 to 31,779 in 1801,[53] and in the poorer-class areas around the booming Port of London. Shadwell and Wapping, where new docks were built in the decade after 1799, were areas of considerable population growth. Southwark, Rotherhithe, Stepney, Bethnal Green, Somers Town, Camden Town, Paddington and Kensington were all districts which required more piped water to serve new buildings and expanding populations. The parish of St Marylebone, north of

Westminster, where both the Chelsea and New River
Companies had mains, developed with particular rapidity
and the houses there were often large and of good quality.
Custom there was indeed a prize worth securing by any water
company, and between 1806 and 1810 the Chelsea
Company spent £30,000 on extending its works and pipes to
enable it to serve Marylebone and the adjacent areas northwards to Paddington.

The companies did not, in general, keep detailed records of
the amount of water they supplied, but from 1787 to 1809
the New River Company recorded the amount of water
pumped by its Boulton and Watt steam engine, this being
required by the manufacturers. The engine raised all the water
supplied by the company to 'the western parts of the town',
and the figures show a considerable increase over the period.
From some 100 million gallons raised in 1790 the amount
increased to 190 million gallons in 1793, 350 million gallons
in 1797 and 450 million gallons in 1806. No consistent pattern of increase can be discerned because of variations in the
area supplied from the Upper Pond, and thus by the engine,
but the upward trend is clear.[54]

Demand for water also increased because of the use of new
appliances and a general increase in cleanliness. The most
important of these appliances was the water closet. Originally
invented in the sixteenth century, it became popular only after
improved versions were patented successively by watchmak-
ers Alexander Cummings and Joseph Bramah in 1775 and
1778 respectively. Bramah's design remained standard for a
century, and he claimed to have made and sold 6,000 closets
by 1797.[55] Fixed baths in numbers were much later in making
their appearance, but in 1809 they were sufficiently numerous for the East London Water Works Company to assess an
additional charge for houses which had such appliances fitted.[56] Water closets and fixed baths required a head of water
to operate effectively, and their introduction, therefore,
increased the likelihood of dissatisfaction with low-pressure
water supplies. If a water closet was to operate on any floor of
a house above the basement, water would have to be carried
from the basement water butt to a cistern on a higher floor.

Another factor making for increased demand for water was
the greater use of easily washable cotton clothing. In 1824
Francis Place, contrasting the present habits of the people of

all classes with what he remembered from his boyhood in the 1780s, wrote that cotton clothes 'were found to be less expensive and as it was necessary to wash them, cleanliness followed as a matter of course ... Cleanliness in matter of dress was necessarily accompanied by cleanliness in other particulars, and this again by the desire to possess more conveniences, and better utensils.'[57] In 1822 Place wrote that the decline of the London death rate in his own lifetime was largely due to 'the change that has taken place ... in the habits of the working classes, who are infinitely more moral and more sober, more cleanly in their persons and their dwellings, than they were formerly ... partly from the success of cotton manufacture.'[58] The enthusiastic commentator who, in 1783, extolled the system of 'buried wooden pipes that supply every house plentifully with water, conducted by leaden pipes into kitchens or cellars, three times a week for the trifling expence of three shillings per quarter'[59] had by 1810 been succeeded by the irritated complainants quoted above.

The water companies, especially the New River Company, were also criticised for being high-handed and arbitrary towards consumers. In 1810 John Johnson, for example, testified that in 1805 he had applied to the New River Company for a supply of water to thirty new houses he owned at Somers Town, and had been told that as the company's existing pipes nearby were inadequate he would have to pay £100 for new services before any supply could be given. There being no other way of obtaining water for his tenants, he had had no option but to pay.[60] The New River Company showed its tyrannical side in the incident of Pocock's Well. For several years before 1809 the Company had been requested to supply water to an increasing number of houses in Holloway and Islington but had neglected to do so, presumably because of the difficulty of supplying areas at a level higher than that of New River Head. In 1809 one George Pocock obtained an Act empowering him to sink a well and pump water from it to Holloway and Islington, but as soon as the Act was passed the New River Company laid pipes through the area 'with great expedition'. The company even pulled down the pump from which the inhabitants had previously obtained their water, thus forcing them to take the New River's supply. The unfortunate Pocock did sink his well, but was unable to meet his costs and went bankrupt in 1815.[61]

Such was London's water supply at the beginning of the nineteenth century. The companies had effected certain improvements in efficiency, notably the progressive introduction of steam engines to raise water and of iron pipes at especially important locations, but these did not directly benefit the consumer. Iron was increasingly available with the great expansion of production during the Revolutionary and Napoleonic Wars and its price was already beginning to fall: but companies which had large amounts of capital tied up in old wooden pipes (the New River Company had 400 miles) were disinclined to expend more on renewing their distribution systems. By the opening years of the century, however, it was likely that if the established companies did not take steps to provide a more regular, higher pressure supply, they would find more powerful competitors than Pocock responding to public demand.

Chapter 2
The newcomers: the establishment of the South London, West Middlesex and East London Water Works Companies, 1805–1810

The established companies were to face successful competition from London's outskirts. The main aim of the new promoters there was at first to supply outlying areas which had no piped water at all, rather than to compete in districts already served: nor did they propose any major departure from the traditional methods of distribution by gravity through wooden pipes. Technical improvements, however, soon enabled them to extend high-pressure supplies into the densely populated central areas.

The first of the new water companies was established in south London, where the most important of the existing concerns, the Lambeth Water Works Company, had been in operation only since 1785, supplying Lambeth with water drawn from the Thames near the site of the present Waterloo Bridge. Southwark was supplied partly by the London Bridge Water Works and partly by the small Borough Water Works, which raised water by means of an atmospheric engine situated at Bankside, near the site that would become the south end of Southwark Bridge. According to an account written in 1835, these two concerns, 'were in a very inefficient state, besides having their pipes running in the same streets, so as to interfere much with each other'.[1] The Lambeth Company, on the other hand, had started with a capital of only £5,590, 'but by careful management, and avoiding a large expenditure at the commencement, a remarkable degree of success attended their enterprise'; the shareholders must have been very patient men, for all profits had been ploughed back into the works rather than distributed as dividends.[2] By 1828 the Company's capital stood at £130,000.[3]

In 1804 proposals for new water works in south-west, north-east and north-west London were made by Ralph Dodd. Dodd, who was born in about 1756, probably in Northumberland, had begun work as a self-styled engineer on the Grand Junction Canal in 1794, after an earlier career as a painter. He had worked on other canals until 1802, mostly in a minor capacity, and had unsuccessfully projected tunnels beneath the Tyne and the Thames.[4] He had no previous experience of water works. His two sons, Barrodale Robert and George, also styled themselves engineers and worked with him. His proposals for new London water companies were set out in his book *Observations on Water*,[5] published in 1805, and containing reports to the subscribers about his intended South London and East London Water Works. It is clear that Dodd planned mainly to supply areas which had not previously had piped water; after listing various parishes he remarked: 'Although all the places above-mentioned may not be wholly destitute of Soft Water, by far the greater part are obliged to depend upon uncertain supplies, and precarious Rains that may fall from the Heavens, take it from stagnated pools, or expensively brought to them by Water Carts.'[6] He proposed to provide a regular, piped supply, which 'possesses the united advantages of administering to our domestic comforts, and ensuring our safety, by extinguishing the devouring Flames that too often invade our dwellings'.[7]

Dodd's South London Water Works was the first to get under way. The inaugural meeting of subscribers was held on 6 October 1804, when it was agreed that a capital of £30,000 should be raised in £100 shares, that a Bill for incorporating the undertaking should be introduced into Parliament, and that Ralph Dodd should be the company's engineer.[8] The required Act was duly obtained, receiving the Royal Assent on 12 July 1805. It empowered the new company to supply water to Camberwell, Lambeth, Bermondsey, Rotherhithe, Deptford, Newington, Walworth, Kennington, Stockwell, Clapham, Peckham Rye, Dulwich, 'and Places adjacent'. Opposition to the Bill by the Lambeth Water Works Company was overcome by inserting a clause which laid down a boundary between the areas to be served by the two companies, and the opposition of various canal companies was removed by a clause prohibiting the company from using its aqueducts as waterways for the carriage of goods or passengers. The Act fixed the company's capital at £50,000 with power to raise a further £30,000 if necessary.

The South London Water Works Company proposed to site its works at Vauxhall Creek, Kennington (the lower stretch of the River Effra), and to raise water by means of a 16 horsepower steam engine to an 'upper tank' 30 feet above ground level.[9] Before any work had started, on 12 August 1805 the Directors reported to the shareholders that 'with regard to Mr. Dodd the Engineer they feel it a Duty to report to the Proprietors with all the delicacy the subject requires they cannot, from all the various Circumstances within their knowledge, recommend his being further employed'. The shareholders duly dismissed Dodd and appointed one Chapman in his place.[10] A long dispute followed over the sum owed to Dodd to cover his expenses as Engineer, which was ultimately settled by arbitration.

Having discarded its originator, the company proceeded to erect its works as planned, and to lay a 12-inch bore iron pipe from its intake to the reservoirs. The traditional wooden pipes, of 3-inch to 7-inch bore, were used for distribution. The works proved to be more expensive and to take longer to construct than had been anticipated, but on 24 June 1807 the first public supplies of water commenced. Disaster then struck: only 56 customers had been obtained when, on 6 August 1807, the engine house, steam engine and upper reservoir were destroyed by a fire believed to have been started deliberately. Although £2,700 fire insurance was paid by the Albion Fire Office, the directors believed that the company had suffered injury to its interests over and above the actual damage because of the delay resulting from the fire.[11] The steam engine was replaced at first by two smaller ones of two and three horsepower respectively, and then, in 1809, by an eight horsepower Trevithick engine.[12] In June 1808 the company still had only 270 customers, and a year later only 525. Although by June 1810 it had laid nearly fifteen miles of wooden pipes and supplied over a thousand consumers, its income was still insufficient for any dividend to be declared, in spite of the relatively high charge of over 30s. per house per annum.[13]

The attitude of the Lambeth Company to its new neighbour appears to have been one of wary benevolence, and relations between the two were reasonably good. When the South London Company's steam engine was destroyed by fire the Lambeth Company immediately offered to supply the 56 customers who had been cut off until the South London was able to resume operations: the offer was regarded as 'friendly and amicable'.[14] The boundary fixed by Parliament between the two companies prevented the South London from encroaching on the Lambeth Company's area, but not the converse. Nevertheless, the Lambeth Company was anxious to avoid any competition, and in December 1807 suspended the laying of its 4-inch pipe in East Lane in order 'to prevent any irritation to the South London Company in the way of competition in that neighbourhood'.[15] In April 1808 the East Lane pipe was taken up, the Lambeth Company 'being of the opinion that a competition would not be to the advantage of either Company'.[16] In 1810, however, the financial difficulties of the South London Company appear to have led its directors to believe that an active competition might prove to be the answer to their problems, and they petitioned Parliament for the repeal of the restrictive clause in their Act. The Bill for this purpose was rejected at the Committee stage, and the statutory boundary remained until 1834.[17] There was no real competition among the water companies south of the Thames until 1839.[18]

The second of the new water companies to be established was much more significant. The West Middlesex Water Works Company was projected by Ralph Dodd in 1804, and its Engineer was his son B.R. Dodd. B.R. Dodd drew up plans during 1805 showing works on Pooles Creek, Fulham, near Walham Green, with an upper reservoir on the north side of Fulham Road,[19] and in 1806 a Bill was presented to Parliament for the incorporation of the new company. Before the House of Lords Committee B.R. Dodd 'proved' the expense of the proposed works as being £23,835, including excavating three reservoirs holding a total of $14\frac{1}{2}$ million gallons, erecting engine houses and laying twelve miles of pipes.[20] The Act was passed in July 1806, and on 12 August a

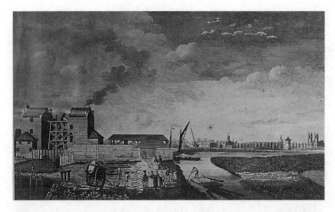

Chelsea Water Works. Now the site of Victoria Railway station.

Board of Directors was appointed by the sixty proprietors named. The Act empowered the Company to raise capital of £80,000 in £100 shares, and to construct works for the purpose of supplying Hammersmith, Chiswick, Brentford and other expanding villages to the west of London, together with 'places adjacent' thereto. The preamble to the Act stated that 'many parts of the said Parishes, Townships and Places are become very populous, and are greatly increased and increasing in Houses and Buildings, and in Cases of Accidents by Fire, the Inhabitants thereof might be exposed to the most calamitous losses for Want of a sufficient supply of Water'. The Act also specifically excluded the Company from supplying any part of the City or Liberties of Westminster or Chelsea, this clause being inserted at the instance of the Chelsea Water Works Company, which feared competition.

Immediately after the passing of the West Middlesex Water Works Act, B.R. Dodd began making preparations for the construction of the works at Pooles Creek. Almost at once the directors expressed a preference for siting the works at Hammersmith instead, and they instructed their Chief Clerk, Robert Sloper, to investigate the legal problems which this would raise. Sloper reported that there were no legal difficulties which could not easily be surmounted, and the directors then purchased plots of land at Hammersmith for £4,500 (compared with the £2,700 allowed in Dodd's estimate for buying land at Pooles Creek). When they instructed B.R. Dodd to prepare estimates for constructing works there, he refused and was suspended, and then, in November 1806, dismissed. William Nicholson,[21] a well-known scientist, was appointed Engineer in his place and agreed that the works should be sited at Hammersmith: he pointed out that this was nearer to the areas to be supplied than was Pooles Creek, which in any case was heavily polluted by land drainage and unfit to be a source of supply. Water would instead be drawn directly from the Thames.[22]

During 1807 the works at Hammersmith were constructed under Nicholson's supervision, being completed by November. They consisted of two reservoirs each holding about 1,300,000 gallons and fed by an intake from the Thames, with two 20 horsepower steam engines to pump from the reservoirs into the mains.[23] The directors resolved to use stone pipes, 'a conveyance by Means of which the Water will be purified, and entirely free from the unpleasant Taste which it is apt to acquire by passing through Wood or Iron', and handbills were distributed extolling the virtues of stone pipes.[24] By the end of 1807, however, when the Stone Pipe Company had proved unable to deliver on time, the directors resolved to use wood or iron instead.[25] John Millington, their Conductor of Works, was asked to report on the relative merits of the two materials. He concluded that the greater cost of iron was more than outweighed by its advantages over wood, principally the longer life and lack of need for maintenance. Iron was stated to cost approximately twice as much as wood, 6 inch iron pipes costing 12s. 6d. per yard compared with 6s. 3d. for wood, but wooden pipes were more expensive to lay because of their larger outer diameter and would not stand up to high pressure. Millington estimated that a mile of iron pipes would cost £1,307 to maintain over a period of 27 years, whereas to maintain a mile of wooden pipes would cost £2,867.10s. On the basis of these calculations the directors decided to use iron pipes only, which they purchased principally from the Butterley Iron Company in Derbyshire.[26] By the middle of 1808 the Company was supplying water to houses in Hammersmith and Chiswick. Nicholson had by that time been replaced as Engineer by Ralph Walker, it being felt that Nicholson's many commitments did not allow him to devote sufficient time to the company's interests. He was, however, retained as a consultant.[27]

Even before the first supplies were available from the West Middlesex Company, the directors were thinking in terms of expansion – but not towards the Middlesex and Surrey villages listed in their Act. At the suggestion of Nicholson, the directors decided to construct a pipeline to a further reservoir at high level on Campden Hill, Kensington, with the object of supplying that part of Marylebone which lay outside the Liberties of Westminster and was thus not prohibited to them by statute. This would involve direct competition with the New River and Chelsea Companies, which already had pipes in Marylebone, although the West Middlesex Directors reckoned in February 1808 that there were 1,200 houses there which were not supplied by either of the old companies.[28] Such direct competition would be something new, as although the old companies did not possess any legal right to a monopoly 'each possessed a monopoly in effect, through the greater part of the district which it supplied. Where their works intermixed, as they often did, it was the effect of a very gradual extension; and though the inhabitants of those parts of the town had the benefit of a choice, no mischievous spirit of rivalry seems to have been excited between the companies'.[29] The directors considered that their iron mains and high-pressure supply (to be pumped by a new 70 horsepower Boulton and Watt engine) would enable them to compete successfully for the high water rents of the prosperous and rapidly-growing areas of Marylebone, Paddington and St Pancras. They concluded that 'the well known extortion and limited power, as to supply, of the New River Company and the bad water and injudicious management of the Chelsea Company render a competition against them, even in the lower or long established part of Marylebone, likely to be very gainful.'[30] During 1808, therefore, the West Middlesex Company secretly purchased land at Kensington (where 2,000 new houses were laid out) and in the following year an 'upper reservoir' was constructed on Campden Hill.

The directors were not averse to seeking powers or property from other companies if this would help their expansionist policies. In December 1807 they approached the Grand Junction Canal Company with a view to purchasing the rights to supply water to Paddington and adjacent areas which that company had had since 1798 but had not yet exercised. The price demanded, £22,000 for a 50-year lease of the rights, was felt to be too high, and negotiations were abandoned in March 1808.[31] A further attempt at expansion followed in November 1809, when the Company offered £20,000 for the York Buildings Water Works Company, which held out for an asking price of £26,000. West Middlesex increased its offer to £22,000, but this was not acceptable to the York Building directors and these negotiations also failed.[32]

The West Middlesex Company, in its early years, went to some lengths to secure public support. The Chelsea and New River Companies were constantly tearing up pavements in order to gain access to leaking wooden pipes, to the annoyance of the public. The West Middlesex Company, on the other hand, was able to assure Commissioners of Paving and the general public that its exclusive use of iron pipes would mean far less frequent repairs and, therefore, far less inconvenience. In April 1808 complaints were received from the Brentford Turnpike Trust that the company's pipe-laying activities had caused the state of the roads to deteriorate, and it promptly carried out repairs. The directors resolved that the Great Western Road, 'already almost unmanageable as to Repairs, should be as little disturbed as possible, by any System of Pipes adopted by this Company', and pointed out to the trustees that 'Iron will last almost in aeternum.'[33] Subsequently, in 1809, the company offered to supply water to the trustees for the purpose of laying the dust on the highways.[34] When the directors were informed that the expense of laying lead communication pipes deterred householders from taking the company's supplies, they resolved that where inhabitants were already supplied by another company 'as an inducement for such to take a supply from this Company, they will at their own expence make such alterations as may be necessary to change the Lead Pipes already laid, from the pipes of other Companies to their own'.[35]

During these years the Company was constantly employing canvassers and distributing handbills to secure custom. The scale of charges adopted by the Company in July 1809 was competitive, if not particularly cheap. The most usual category of house, paying a rental of up to £30 per annum, was to pay water rents of 5% of the annual rental, subject to a minimum of 10s. a year. Houses with a rental of over £40 were to pay 4%. Additional charges were to be made of three guineas for a fixed bath, half a guinea for a water closet, 15s. for a one or two-stall stable, and 10s. if a carriage was kept.[36]

The West Middlesex Company's new reservoir at Kensington was opened on 4 December 1809 in a ceremony attended by a detachment of the Kensington Volunteers. Lord Cochrane, George Byng, Sir Francis Burdett and William Mellish, all Members of Parliament, were invited as guests on honour.[37] By that time the company's plans for expanding its activities into the area already supplied by the Chelsea Company had run into opposition from the influential Marylebone Select Vestry, which feared that the entry of another water company into the parish would mean great destruction of the pavements, and doubts were raised as to whether the company could legally enter any part of Marylebone. Counsel's opinion was sought, and the directors decided that it would be advisable to obtain a new Act of Parliament in order to remove the restrictive clause in the Act of 1806.[38]

A new West Middlesex Water Works Bill was introduced into Parliament in the session of 1810, supported by petitions which the company had secured from inhabitants of Marylebone, Westminster and other districts: the company's Chief Clerk reported to the Directors that 'it is most true that no Bill ever appeared in the House of Commons supported by a more powerful Body of Petitions'.[39] Support was also canvassed and obtained from the Fire Offices, with promises that the company's iron mains would be kept full of water at all times. Even the Marylebone Select Vestry was persuaded to support the Bill – the directors had issued instructions in November 1809 that for the time being pipe-laying in Marylebone should be done only in unpaved streets.[40] The agreement of the Chelsea Company, however, was not forthcoming. The battle between the rival companies was fought out before the Commons and Lords Committees, and the stream of witnesses produced by the West Middlesex Company, testifying to the 'scanty and insufficient' supply provided by the old companies to Marylebone, carried the day.[41] Valuable support was given by George Byng and the Dukes of Bedford and Portland, the two Dukes having much property in the area of London concerned. Unexpected opposition was encountered in the House of Lords from the Grand Junction Canal Company, but, in the words of the West Middlesex Company's Chief Clerk, the proprietors 'were possessed of

York Buildings Water Works. The site of the old York Buildings Works, seen here in about 1780, is close to that of the present Charing Cross Station.

firmness enough to determine on an energetic resistance against the Extortion and Oppression which was attempted and threatened', and the contest resulted in the 'discomfiture and disgrace' of the objectors.[42] The West Middlesex Water Works Act duly received the Royal Assent in May 1810.

The new Act gave the Company power to raise an additional £160,000 capital (the original £80,000 having all been raised and expended), raised the limit on the number of shares held by any individual from 20 to 50, and removed the boundary laid down by the Act of 1806. The company was, therefore, empowered to supply houses in the whole of Marylebone and Westminster, and to raise the funds which would enable it to do so. The Act also forbade the Company to sell its rights of supply to any other company, compelled it to lay mains in certain streets and to keep them full of water for security against fire, and, while recognising the principle of fair competition, prohibited it from 'hindering or obstructing' the New River, Chelsea and York Buildings Companies. The scene was thus set for a vigorous competition among water companies in the western part of London. The West Middlesex Directors were in no doubt as to the rightness of their policy: in November 1809, when announcing to their shareholders their intention to compete against the 'monopolistic' Chelsea Company, they declared that 'the struggle against an attempt at Monopoly will add additional Lustre to the Patriotic

Exertions of the Individuals who have so liberally advanced
their Capital in this most Important Public Undertaking'.[43]

Meanwhile, on the other side of London, the third of the
new water companies conceived by Ralph Dodd had taken
shape. This was the East London Water Works Company,
whose early history followed a somewhat similar course to
that of the West Middlesex Company (the two had many proprietors and some directors in common). Dodd's original proposals in 1805 provided for a lower reservoir to be
constructed at Old Ford on the lower Lee, sited so that it
would be filled by the action of the tide flowing up the
Thames, and for water 'after sufficiently settling and filter'd, to
be forced through Iron Pipes to a summit Reservoir' by a
steam engine.[44] Dodd was confident that 'a very handsome
Profit will accrue to the Share-holders, for their capital
advanced in this desirable Undertaking; which profits will be
of a perpetual and increasing nature, from various improvements and New Buildings which are continually erecting,
which will doubtless need a supply of Water'. He pointed out
that 'in the three Parishes of Bethnal Green, Hackney and
Tottenham only, are upwards of 15,000 Houses'.[45]
Subscriptions were obtained, including one from the celebrated East End brewers, Truman, Hanbury & Co., and a Bill was
introduced into Parliament in the 1807 session. The now
familiar figure of Ralph Dodd, squeezed out of the South
London and West Middlesex concerns, reappeared as the East
London Company's Engineer. He deposited a plan showing
mains extending from Old Ford northwards through Hackney,
Dalston, Stoke Newington, Clapton, Stamford Hill and
Tottenham, westwards to Bethnal Green, Islington and
Holloway and through the City as far as St Paul's, and south-
wards to Bow, Stepney and Mile End.[46] Most of the areas con-
cerned were outside the districts served by the New River
Company, which, however, already supplied the City and part
of Islington. The main opposition to the Bill came from the
London Dock Company, which owned the old Shadwell and
West Ham water works.[47]

The East London Water Works Act became law in August
1807 and the first General Assembly of Proprietors was held
on 13 August. Already, as in the case of the South London
Company, Ralph Dodd had been dismissed as Engineer, this
time after quarrelling with the directors. Ralph Walker, who

was later to become Engineer to the West Middlesex
Company, was appointed in his place. Dodd having been disposed of, the Company proceeded to construct the Old Ford
works and to lay pipes to the surrounding districts. One of the
first steps was to open negotiations with the London Dock
Company for the purchase of the Shadwell and West Ham
works; the purchase was made in January 1808 for
£130,000, payable in instalments.[48] The high price necessi-
tated another Act of Parliament being obtained in the 1808
session to empower the Company to raise the required additional capital. The next decision to be made was the material
of the pipes to be used, and the Engineer initially recommended that while iron pipes should be used for mains, to avoid the
need for parallel lines of wooden pipes, the services should be
of wood. Walker held that 'neither Public nor private Bodies
ought to run any risk by trying new experiments or Inventions
in the first Instance',[49] and in accordance with this belief the
Directors decided not to try the stone pipes which were offered
at competitive prices by the Patent Stone Pipe Manufactory.[50]

Walker surveyed the Shadwell and West Ham works in
March 1808, and recommended that the first extensions of
mains from them should be towards Bethnal Green, which 'is
also the situation, where the greatest number of Houses are in
want of water. In Bethnal Green and Stepney 1,500 houses
may soon be added to the supply'. He felt that 'little or no danger is to be apprehended from the New River Company carrying their supply to the Eastward, first because of the increase
of first and second rate houses of the West End of Town will
pay better than those to the Eastward, and secondly because
in the dry seasons of the year … they are unable to give satisfaction to their present customers particularly to Brewers,
Dyers &c.'[51] Despite this, in April 1808 an anonymous share-
holder warned the directors that 'It is the determination of the
New River Company to surround and encompass the East
London Water Works every way possible in order to injure the
concern as far as in their power to do',[52] and in June the directors decided to extend their mains to Limehouse as soon as
possible in order to forestall any moves in that direction by
their rivals. In East London, therefore, there were early indica-
tions that competition was likely to develop. An unofficial
approach from the New River Company in June 1808, with a
view to agreeing a boundary between the two companies,

came to nothing.[53]

The East London Company bought some wooden pipes in 1808, but Walker then apparently changed his mind and advised that the services should instead be of iron. After a careful comparison of the current prices of iron, wooden and stone pipes in August 1808 the directors decided to use iron only.[54] and in April 1809 Walker reported that 'The more I see of the daily failures of wooden Pipes and the labour and expence of keeping the Mains and Services of your Shadwell and West Ham Works in repair the more I am convinced of the utility and advantages to be ultimately derived by the Company from the adoption of Iron Pipes.'[55]

Iron pipes were bought mainly from the Butterley Iron Company and from Booth and Company of Sheffield, but difficulties of transport (by canal from Derbyshire or Yorkshire to the east coast, then by sea to London) during the winter of 1808–9 caused delays and irritation. Walker was despatched in January 1809 to the manufacturers in order to speed up deliveries, and in August it was necessary for him to go to Sheffield again for the same purpose.[56] Despite these delays, more than 12½ miles of iron pipes had already been laid by June 1809, including pipes through Bishopsgate, Aldgate and Spitalfields encroaching on the areas of the New River Company and London Bridge Water Works.[57] Iron pipes continued to be laid as fast as they could be obtained, and by the time that the Old Ford works were completed in October 1809 some 20 miles of pipes had been laid.[58] Until this date the customers so far obtained by the company were supplied from the old works at West Ham and Shadwell, whose power to serve an increased number of consumers was limited, but with the completion of the Old Ford works a great extension of the company's operations became possible.

The Old Ford works were opened on 23 October 1809 in an impressive ceremony. The Duke of Cambridge was to have attended as guest of honour, but was unable to be present owing to the illness of his sister, Princess Amelia. The ceremony was graced by the presence of the Lord Mayor of London, the Chairman of the Honourable East India Company and William Mellish, MP, and there was a stand for spectators, 'filled with beauty and fashion'. The bands of the First Tower Hamlets Militia and the Loyal Bow Volunteers played God Save the King, Rule Britannia, Water Parted from the Sea 'and other popular and appropriate airs', royal salutes were fired and the Union Flag was displayed. The Rev. Edward Robson preached a sermon on the text 'Behold, I will stand before thee there upon the rock in Horeb; and thou shalt smite the rock, and there shall come water out of it, that the people may drink' to 'return thanks to the Supreme Being for the power thereby vested in the Company of dispensing to the numerous Inhabitants of the Eastern District of the Metropolis the Blessings of Health, Security and Domestic Comfort'. To the sound of Bow Bells, the Lord Mayor opened the sluices to fill the reservoir 'amidst the cheering and Acclamations of several Thousands of Spectators', the whole ceremony being 'unattended by the smallest Accident'. The motto adopted for the new works was a quote from Horace: *Fies Nobilium Tu Quoque Fontium* ('You too will become one of the renowned springs'). The proceedings terminated with a grand dinner at the City of London Tavern, costing 15s. per head.[59] (For comparison, the labourers at the Shadwell works were paid wages of 13s. per week.)

The energetic expansion of the East London and West Middlesex Companies had thus, by 1810, given notice that competition in both eastern and western London was about to begin in earnest. Only south of the river were relations between the old and new water companies amicable.

Chapter 3
Competition 1810–1815

By the end of 1809 the West Middlesex Company was supplying water to houses in its original area of Hammersmith,
Brentford and Chiswick, and had recently begun to lay mains
into Marylebone and Paddington. In November 1809 the
directors reported to the general assembly of shareholders that
they were 'determined to possess the North Western District'
and that the supply of some houses in Paddington and
Marylebone had already been obtained.[1] The Company's Act
of 1810, removing the previous statutory boundary with the
Chelsea Company's area, opened up further opportunities for
expansion which were quickly seized. By May 1811 the company considered that it had 'taken possession of the very flourishing District of Chelsea', although allowance must be made
for exaggeration here, for the figure proudly given was of 400
houses already laid on 'or promised by builders'.[2] At the same
time there was expansion eastwards, into the area previously
served exclusively by the New River Company: an 18-inch
main was being laid in Tottenham Court Road. By November
1811 the company was supplying a total of 1,033 houses,
rising to 2,053 by May 1812 and 4,155 by May 1813. To
obtain these customers it was necessary for the Company to
lay mains and services through almost the whole of western
London; by early 1813 its pipes were being laid through St
Giles, Bloomsbury and the great new Bedford Estate there,
and in the second half of 1813 fourteen miles of iron pipes
were laid in the Marylebone Park development alone. In 1814
the company extended northwards, laying mains along Euston
Street, into Somers Town and the Battle Bridge Estate, and
north-westwards along the Hampstead Road to the St John's
Wood Estate.

This extensive and costly network of iron pipes was accompanied by great efforts to obtain public support. For example, in October 1811 an advertisement was placed in all the London newspapers for three weeks, saying that competition always reduces prices and that the West Middlesex Company 'can supply the Parish of St Marylebone and its neighbourhood with Water of the purest quality, unlimited in quantity, and delivered, if chosen, in the upper Stories of the loftiest Houses in London'.[3] The company thus asserted its advantages to the public in terms of water quality, cheapness and convenience, as compared with its established rivals. The same message was subsequently given by handbills distributed throughout Marylebone and Paddington.

In November 1812 the West Middlesex Company scored a useful propaganda point as a result of a fire at the Pantheon Theatre. Early in 1812 two large cisterns had been constructed at the top of the theatre as security against fire, an early example of the modern type of fire protection. The Pantheon's example was followed by the Drury Lane and Covent Garden theatres. On 17 November 1812 the Pantheon Theatre caught fire, and the damage was greatly restricted by the immediate availability of water to douse the flames. The West Middlesex Company took great credit for this happy outcome: in an advertisement in the press it pointed out that the Pantheon's fire cisterns were served by its high-pressure supply, which was thus responsible for the preservation of the theatre and the surrounding houses. Attention was thus drawn to 'the superior power of their works, constructed on principles in which the great improvements of modern science are brought into action'.[4]

By November 1815, the West Middlesex Company had by immense exertions secured nearly 7,000 customers. On the other side of London, the East London Water Works Company expanded on a grander scale in terms of number of houses supplied and length of mains laid. Starting with the base of the old West Ham and Shadwell works, which between them served some 10,000 houses (mostly of the poorer sort) on the eastern fringes of London, the company was able to start a programme of energetic expansion once its Old Ford works were completed in October 1809. It had already laid some iron mains into the City around Aldgate, Bishopsgate and Spitalfields, and now extended its system in all directions with great rapidity. Pipes were laid northwards through Hackney to Homerton and Clapton, southwards to Limehouse and Poplar, while the greatest efforts were concentrated westwards, in the densely-populated areas of Bethnal Green, Stepney, Whitechapel, Shoredith and the City. In March 1810 an 'ocular demonstration' was given in Spitalfields of the 'immense power' of the Company's works, a jet of water being emitted to a height of fifty feet, and as a direct result several very valuable customers were obtained. Messrs. Racine and Jacques, dyers, for example, agreed to pay sixty guineas a year for a supply, and Hanbury & Co, brewers, took a supply for £30 per year.[5] The length of iron mains laid by the East London Company increased from 20 miles in October 1809 to 30 miles in March 1810, 54 miles in March 1811 and 67½ miles in October 1812. By the latter date the Company had 21,000 customers (including the 10,000 or so inherited from the West Ham and Shadwell works), and was still expanding.[6]

While the two new companies were busily extending their operations, a third was added to their number in 1811, as an off-shoot of a large canal company. In 1798 the Grand Junction Canal Company had obtained powers to supply water to Paddington and adjacent areas from its canal, and in 1810 leased these powers to a group of men also connected with the Stone Pipe Manufactory, the most prominent of them being Samuel Hill. These men had failed to persuade the East London and West Middlesex Companies to adopt stone pipes (except to a very limited extent as experiments) and now, it appears, decided to set up their own water works company to act as an outlet for their pipes. The Grand Junction Water Works Company was incorporated by an Act of 1811, with £150,000 capital in £50 shares. Samuel Hill was a director, and the services of the celebrated John Rennie were obtained as Engineer. The works were to consist of two reservoirs at Paddington, filled with water from the Grand Junction Canal, with a 42-inch main iron pipe from the canal to the reservoirs, and two 70-horsepower Boulton and Watt steam engines to pump water from the reservoirs down a 30-inch main leading to Oxford Street and Drury Lane.[7] The Company, therefore, intended to compete directly with the West Middlesex Company as well as the established New River and Chelsea Companies, and its operations were to be on a large scale. In July 1811 the Company commended itself to the public, by handbill and newspaper advertisement, in the following terms:

The Directors of the Company feel it their duty respectfully to inform the Public that these Works will be enabled to supply a body of Water three times greater, and in a more pure and brilliant state, than has yet been effected, and that the elevated situation of the Reservoirs, being 86 feet above high Water mark, the magnitude of the principal Main, and the great powers of the Engines, will raise the Water into the upper parts of the Houses, without the great expence and continual Labor of forcing Pumps, for the supply of Baths, Water Closets, Laundries, and other domestic purposes of necessary use, health and pleasure, and that in cases of Fire, the body of Water in constant readiness, as well in the Mains, as in the Cisterns at the tops of Individual Houses, will be so great as to prevent the dreadful progress hitherto frequently made,before even a moderate supply could be furnished.[8]

The importance attached to the new technology represented by the very large cast iron pipes and the powerful steam engines is significant. Despite the stress laid on the purity and brilliance of the water to be supplied, Rennie did not consider it necessary to filter the water at the Paddington reservoir. He felt that 'the Water may sufficiently deposit all its impurity in that Reservoir without filtration'.[9]

In July 1811, before the reservoirs or engine-house had been constructed, the Grand Junction Company ordered 72,000 yards of pipes from the Stone Pipe Company. The directors considered it as 'a measure of expediency on behalf of this Company and of justice to the Stone Pipe Company if this Undertaking should be extended as far and as rapidly as may be hoped for, so as to require an extension of the present Contract before it may be completed'.[10] The utmost confidence was felt in the suitability of the stone pipes: when the Marylebone Select Vestry expressed concern, in September 1811, about the possible damage to pavements caused by leaking stone pipes, the directors replied that there was no cause for alarm.[11] The first of the large steam engines was commissioned in April 1812, and 828 yards of 42-inch iron main was laid from the canal to the Paddington reservoirs by June 1812. The 30-inch main had by that time been laid as far as Bond Street, and 6,409 yards of stone pipes were in the ground. The stone pipes, however, were not performing as well under pressure as had been anticipated, several failures having occurred. In July 1812, after a report from Rennie, the

directors resolved that 'the use of Stone Pipes for Mains cannot be continued with', and a week later Rennie reported that
'from the trials already made he has great doubts of the effectual and lasting use of Stone Service Pipes'.[12] The directors
decided to order iron pipes to replace the stone, but were
reluctant to abandon the stone pipes entirely until further tests
proved conclusively that they were completely unsuitable for
use with high-pressure supplies. On 5 March 1813 it was
resolved 'That this Company determine to have nothing further to do with Stone Pipes.'[13]

The delay caused by the Grand Junction Company's unfortunate experiment with stone pipes had, as Rennie pointed
out, 'allowed time for other Water Works Companies to get
possession of the supply'.[14] It was not until late in 1812 that
the company began supplying water; by early December, however, nearly 11,000 yards of iron pipes had been laid and the
first 100 houses were receiving supplies in Paddington. By
April 1813 some 400 houses were in supply, mainly in the
parishes of Marylebone and St George's Hanover Square, and
by the end of 1813 the company had nearly 1,400 customers. At the end of 1815 it had a network of mains and services through Marylebone, Westminster and Chelsea and
supplied 2,776 houses from some 40 miles of iron pipes.[15]

Another competitor for the water rents of the west end of
London appeared in the shape of the York Buildings Company.
This company, as noted in the first chapter, had been supplying water to a small area of Westminster for over a century; it
had shed the numerous other interests it had acquired early in
the eighteenth century, and its chief claim to distinction was
to have been the first London water company to install a
steam engine. In late 1809, after the failure of negotiations for
a take-over by the West Middlesex Company, a group of shareholders in the West Middlesex and East London Companies
(including the West Middlesex chairman) bought the York
Buildings works and network of wooden mains. According to
the Company Secretary, these gentlemen 'conceived that by
changing the complete system, which they did ... they could
realise a very large rental'.[16] To this end, they raised £75,000
capital in 1810, doubled it in 1812, and expended the whole
in laying a system of iron mains through an area much larger
than that reached by the company's old wooden pipes.[17]

By 1812, then, the old New River, Chelsea and London

Water main crossing the Fleet River. This classic scene illustrates both the nature of early nineteenth-century water mains – parallel rows of wooden pipes – and the substantial leakage from them even at low pressure.

Bridge Companies were under serious attack The New River Company faced challenges from the East London Company in the east and from the West Middlesex, Grand Junction and newly-aggressive York Buildings Companies in the west, where the Chelsea Company also found itself facing competition. The new companies all used most vigorous methods to promote their expansion and discredit their rivals: they did not hesitate to condemn, in the name of competition, the 'monopolies' which they alleged to have been enjoyed by the old companies, while resisting the establishment of more new companies which might threaten their own positions.

In June 1809 the East London Company's Committee of Works submitted to the directors that 'it was material to the Interest of this Company to omit no opportunity of creating a Competition in favour of the Company', [18] and this became the Company's guiding principle during the next few years. Already, the London Bridge Water Works had protested that East London pipes were being laid within the London Bridge limit of supply, at Aldgate, and the answer was given that the East London Company had the power to lay mains in that district and intended to exercise it.[19] The method of competition was to stress cost, offering to supply houses at a charge lower than that made by the old companies. The company's workmen frequently damaged lead pipes leading from the New River company's services to customers' houses, this damage eliciting complaints in March, June and July 1810, and its frequency led to suspicions that it was not always accidental. In July 1810 the New River Company expressed concern at 'the extraordinary Conduct of the East London Water Company in their efforts to induce this companys Tenants to take that companys Water',[20] and in February 1811 held a special meeting of directors to consider measures 'to counteract the means now employing by the Proprietors of the East London Water Works to deprive this Company of their Tenants and which have already succeeded to a considerable extent'.[21] The measures decided upon were to reduce rates to customers where the East London had made offers, to instruct collectors to canvass customers for support, and to advertise by means of posters, handbills and the press.[22]

Despite these efforts, the New River Company lost many customers to the East London over the next few years, and the general level of charges in the area affected fell considerably. For example, until February 1812 a Mr. Leary paid £10 a year for a supply to his twenty houses in New Inn Yard, Curtain Road; he then informed the New River Company that the East London had offered to supply him for £8, and the New River accordingly reduced his charges to match.[23] Mrs. Woodzell's rent of £6.14s. for twelve houses in Shoreditch was reduced to £4 in April 1812,[24] and in July the New River Company reduced its charges for supplies to Broad Street Buildings by twenty per cent to counteract East London offers.[25] By 1813, the East London Company was refusing to supply houses in the areas where it had an exclusive supply unless the owners agreed to take its water for any houses they owned in the competition area: in April 1815 it cut off the supply from four houses in Bethnal Green because the owner had changed to the New River Company in respect of fourteen tenements which he owned in Whitechapel.[26] In general, great confusion was caused in eastern London by the competition. With both companies having mains in the same streets in many cases, customers were able to reduce their charges for water by constantly changing from one to the other, and sometimes were able to avoid payment of arrears each time.[27]

The New River Company experienced similar problems on the other side of its district in the West End. There the West Middlesex, Grand Junction and York Buildings Companies were all attempting to expand at the expense of the two old-established companies, using the same methods as did the East London. The West Middlesex was the greatest threat to the New River Company; once again, water charges had to be reduced to counteract the newcomer's offers, and 'accidental' damage to lead communication pipes was frequent. The New River Company's collectors were busy here too in visiting customers to seek their support; in September 1812, for example, a special effort was put into canvassing at Tottenham Court Road.[28] More sinister methods on the part of the West Middlesex were also suspected. In March 1812 it was reported that West Middlesex workmen were breaking New River customers' lead pipes 'and leave them unrepaired for a fortnight, during which time the Tenants are without Water'; letters of complaint were sent to the company.[29] In September 1812 a West Middlesex plumber 'maliciously' stopped up the lead pipe serving 41 Middlesex Street with clay, and the New River Company felt it necessary to threaten prosecution.[30] In January 1813 the New River directors recorded their suspicions that the damage so often done to their lead and wooden pipes by the West Middlesex workmen was intentional.[31] In February 1813 the New River turncock in Somers Town, it was reported, 'had done the Company great Injury with their Tenants in not well supplying them with water', and the New River inspector 'had reason to think he had been tampered with by the Servants of the West Middlesex Company'. The turncock was dismissed.[32] The West Middlesex Company was also in the habit of changing the supply to houses from the New River or Chelsea Company's mains to its own without the owners' consent (generally with the connivance of servants who were no doubt rewarded), then collecting water rents. The owners were thus presented with demands for payment from more than one company. Examples of this occurring were that of Colonel Mercer at 48 Queen Anne Street in February 1813 and that of Mr Grant at 15 Upper Gower Street in September. In Colonel Mercer's case, the servants refused to

SIR,

BEING ordered by the NEW RIVER COMPANY to wait on you to counteract mis-representations that are industriously circulated to their prejudice, I take the liberty of requesting, you will have the goodness, if any applications should be made to induce you to change your supply of Water, not to consent thereto until I have had an opportunity of seeing you : I am directed also to say, that whatever apparent advantages may be held out to you, the NEW RIVER COMPANY are determined to make a sacrifice, and meet their opponents on any terms they may offer.

I am,.

SIR,

Your obedient humble Servant,

Collector.

7th November, 1811.

Handbill 1 – New River Company, 1811. The New River Company offers to reduce its rates to fend off competition.

let the New River collector see the Colonel, increasing suspicions of their collusion.[33] The West Middlesex directors were entitled to record, in November 1813, that 'every exertion has been made against our opponents the New River Company'.[34]

The York Buildings Company, under its new ownership, was equally aggressive. Not only did its workmen damage New River pipes and illicitly change tenants' supplies to its own mains, but they resorted to a night shift for the purpose. In December 1811, for example, a New River collector saw

York Buildings workmen changing the supply to 6 Craven Street, Strand before daylight, and 6 and 7 George Street were changed in the same way.[35] On enquiry to the tenants, the New River Company established that no authority had been given for the changes, and the supplies were reconnected to the New River services. In August 1812 York Buildings workmen laying pipes in Blue Cross Street cut the lead pipe serving Mrs Hughes (a New River customer) and 'told her she should not have any water unless she consented to have it from their Company'.[36] The New River directors were constantly sending letters of complaint to the York Buildings Company about these incidents.

The Grand Junction Company also competed against the New River Company, which recorded in alarm in February 1817 that Grand Junction employees were canvassing as far east as Leather Lane and Saffron Hill,[37] and also against the Chelsea and West Middlesex Companies. The usual complaints were made against the Grand Junction of illicit changes of supply, for example at Piccadilly in August 1814 (New River), and Smiths Rents, York Street in July 1815. Although the Grand Junction was the latecomer, it had an advantage over the New River and Chelsea Companies in its 'high service' (in July 1814 it was able to offer supplies 'to the tops of the houses' in High Holborn at rates twenty per cent below the New River Company's existing charges[38]), and over all the other companies in its 'constant supply'. Throughout the period of the competition the Grand Junction was the only company to boast that its services, as well as mains, were always full of water so that customers could obtain water at any time.

The established companies strenuously resisted the loss of their customers, and allegations of malpractice were not all one way. In May 1813, for instance, the West Middlesex Company protested that a New River collector had alleged to customers that the West Middlesex was insolvent, and that if the customers changed the New River would charge them double or treble rates when they had to change back. The New River directors replied that no authority had been given to defame any other company, but 'They think that if the origin of these mutual complaints was looked out, it would not appear that the first cause of them was with the servants of the New River Company.'[39] In April 1813 the West Middlesex complained that a New River turncock was following West Middlesex employees who were soliciting custom, 'shouting and using gross and insulting Language';[40] in December 1814 they alleged that New River workmen had damaged a West Middlesex pipe in Seymour Place, causing No. 6 to be flooded.[41] The most acrimonious exchange of correspondence occurred in January 1815 and began with a routine complaint that New River workmen had changed the supply to 74 Gower Street from the West Middlesex service to their own, without the consent of the owner, Mrs Lloyd. It appears from the subsequent exchange of letters that the rival companies' workmen had fought each other in the street. The matter was eventually resolved when the West Middlesex Company's Secretary, Matthias Koops Knight, personally called on Mrs Loyd to ascertain her wishes, and she supported his version of events; the New River collector concerned was ordered to visit the West Middlesex offices to apologise, and relations between the two companies became more cordial.[42]

The Chelsea Company attempted to stop the southward expansion of the Grand Junction Company by applying to the Lord Chancellor for an injunction restraining the Grand Junction from supplying 'any part of the City and Liberties of Westminster' with water. The Lord Chancellor heard the case in December 1814 and, after hearing evidence as to the relative cost and efficiency of the old and new supplies, refused the injunction and granted costs to the Grand Junction Company.[43] The Chelsea Company then tried persuading the St Mary's Westminster Paving Committee to prohibit the Grand Junction's breaking up the pavements for pipe-laying, 'but on the contrary one of the Committee expressed a wish that Westminster was better supplied as he had been eight days without a drop of Water from the Chelsea Company'.[44] The expansion of the new companies into the Chelsea and New River districts continued unabated.

The effects of the competition on the established water companies were little short of disastrous. The number of houses supplied by the New River Company fell from 59,000 in 1809 to 54,000 in 1814, and the amount received in water rents fell from £81,000 to £64,000 over the same period.[45] At the same time, the company's expenses rose as it was necessary to start laying iron pipes in place of wood, work steam engines more frequently to keep up the high service in order to

compete, and pay officials to canvass energetically. The effect
on dividends was catastrophic. During the period 1789–1810
an average dividend of £450 per New River share was paid
each year. In 1812 only £220 per share was paid, in 1813
£113 and in 1814 £23: the result of this sharp fall was to
reduce many of the proprietors to 'a state of the most
deplorable indigence'.[46] Chelsea Company dividends continued at the rate of 12s. per share per annum, but the reserve of
£40,000 which had been accumulated by 1810 had to be
expended during the competition period as expenditure con-
sistently exceed income. The worst affected of the old companies was the London Bridge Water Works. In January 1812
the Secretary reported that 'within the last Six Months a considerable number of Tenants who had for many Years been in
the habit of taking their Water from these Works had changed
their Pipes to the East London Water Works, and he was fear-
ful that Several more might be induced ... to discontinue their
Supply from these Works'. Handbills were circulated in the
Bishopsgate area, asking for loyalty to the Company, but losses of custom continued.[47] The New River Company, it was
noted in November 1812, 'have endeavoured in some measure to make good their loss, by attempting to seduce the
Inhabitants of the internal parts of the City who take their
Water from these Works to receive it from them, by Offers to
Serve them at a lower Rate, whilst the East London Water
Works are making similar Offers in the Out Parts.'[48] The 'most
ungenerous Conduct' of the New River Company in this
respect continued: in 1816 the London Bridge Committee
recorded that 'through their misrepresentations they have in
some instances been successful'.[49] In 1812 the London
Bridge Water Works found it necessary to reduce its annual
dividend from £3 to £2.10s. per share, and had to sell
£5,000 worth of stock to meet current expenses.[50]

   All the old companies, then, found the period of competition a financial strain. So did the new companies. The general
reduction in the levels of water rents meant that they realised
much smaller returns than had been anticipated, and all of
them had seriously underestimated the amount of capital
required to construct their works and lay their networks of
mains and services. The West Middlesex Company's capital,
originally fixed in 1806 at £80,000, had by 1813 increased
to £340,000, the East London Company's reached

£380,000, and the Grand Junction Company's, in 1811 fixed at £150,000, was increased in 1813 to £300,000 (of which £240,000 was actually raised). In all three cases the original proprietors confidently expected large and increasing dividends almost immediately, but in fact dividends were small and in some cases non-existent. The East London Company paid a 1% dividend in 1808, 4% in 1809, 7% in 1810, 1% in 1811, 2% in 1812, nothing in 1813–14, and 2% in 1815–16. The West Middlesex Company paid no dividends at all between 1810 and 1819, and the Grand Junction Company none from its foundation in 1811 until 1819. Share prices fluctuated according to the public perception of the companies' prospects. West Middlesex shares were sold at par until September 1809, then at premiums of £10 – £45 up to March 1810, the prices rising to £125 premium by June 1810. They then began to fall in price, being down to £20 premium by December 1810 and back to par by July 1811. The fall continued to £15 discount in late 1811, £60 discount in November 1812, £74 discount in November 1813 and £88 discount – selling price of a mere £12 for a £100 share – in early 1814.[51] The prices of the East London Company's shares showed a similar pattern: they reached £130 premium in 1810, then fell fairly steadily to a nadir of £45 discount by 1815.[52] The East London Company, which had suffered 'great and serious inconvenience' from persons 'who availed themselves of the Competition with other Companies to attempt to unduly lower the rates and in some cases evading payment for a long time',[53] economised by dismissing their Superintendents of Turncocks (April 1813) and restricting the use of their steam engines for pumping.[54]

The West Middlesex Company's financial problems were more severe. Among its projects was an agreement concluded early in 1812 with the Commissioners of Woods and Forests for the exclusive right to supply the large number of houses to be built in Marylebone Park;[55] part of the agreement was an undertaking to build an ornamental basin in the Park.[56] By September 1812, however, the directors realised that they could not afford the £18,000 which the basin was estimated to cost, and asked to be released from this clause. The Commissioners would not agree, and threatened that if the company did not comply the government would oppose its Bill (which sought powers to raise additional capital) in the next parliamentary session. The company had to accept this ultimatum, but when the new Act passed in 1813 and additional shares were offered for sale, no purchasers could be found at a price of more than £30 for a nominal £100 share. Only £74,000 of the intended £120,000 could eventually be raised, and plans to raise £20,000 more by loans and mortgages failed. The government eventually realised that the company was incapable of fulfilling its engagement and released it from the ornamental basin contract in November 1813.[57] By 1814 the Company's outstanding debts reached £96,000, and although stringent economies succeeded in reducing them to £45,000 by the following May, in August 1815 it was calculated that debts exceeded disposable assets by £17,000.[58] The directors, who had felt compelled to waive their fees in the interests of economy, were clearly right in their opinion as to the competition with the New River Company: in September 1815 they reported that 'little or no prospect whatever appeared of any real or substantial benefit being derived, while the two Companies remained in a state of hostile Competition'.[59]

The Grand Junction Company had special problems of its own, in addition to those suffered in common with the other companies. There was a long dispute with the Stone Pipe Company, which was concluded by the latter surrendering Grand Junction shares to the value of some £22,000 (out of a total of £33,000 expended on stone pipes), and this involved the resignation of two Grand Junction directors who were also on the board of the Stone Pipe Company.[60] The source of the Grand Junction's water supply also caused trouble. The company had constructed a reservoir at Ruislip, fed by the Rivers Brent and Colne, whence the water was carried along the Grand Junction Canal to the settling reservoirs at Paddington. In December 1813 it assured the Commissioners of Hans Town, who were considering taking supplies from the company, that 'The sources ... afforded a conviction that the Grand Junction supply and that their means can never fail, that they must give to their Tenants an unceasing supply because the Pipes are always full, the Water is always on and as it is constantly coming in it must always be fresh.'[61] In early 1814, however, a 'sudden irruption of foul water from Brent Feeder into the canal' discoloured the water, caused many complaints from consumers and effectively stopped expansion for a time by exciting prejudice among the public.[62] No sooner had this problem been overcome than floods in 1815 and 1816 caused further discolouration, and the company even considered filtering its water.[63] This extreme step was found to be unnecessary, but the company had to construct a new feeder to the Ruislip reservoir so that its supply came exclusively from the River Colne.[64] Under the circumstances it is not surprising that expansion was slow, with only 2,882 houses being supplied by June 1816. In that month the half-yearly General Assembly of proprietors was informed that the increase was very small, 'there having been for want of funds no extension of the Works since the last General Meeting'.[65] Income in that year was £4,625, which just balanced the 'ordinary expenditure' but provided no return at all on the £240,000 invested capital.

By 1815 it was becoming clear to all the water companies that the competition was benefiting none of them, and that unless prompt action were taken to end it some at least of them would soon face financial collapse.

Chapter 4
Agreement 1815–1818

The eventual solution to the problems raised by competition
was reached between 1815 and 1818. The weaker companies went to the wall, while the others made a series of agreements leaving each with an exclusive area of supply. The first
serious negotiations were opened between the East London
and New River companies as early as May 1813, when the
East London directors pointed out to the New River Company
that 'great advantage is taken by many persons residing in the
District where the New River Company and this Company are
in competition by frequently changing from one to the other,
seeking unduly to lower the Rates, and in many instances
evading the payment of them altogether'.[1] They suggested
that a mutually agreed boundary between the two companies
would be the answer, this proposal indicating that they
already realised that rivalry would not ensure prosperity. The
New River Company, however, was not yet prepared to abandon any part of its area and merely suggested that each company should ensure that intending customers were not in debt
to the other before agreeing to give supplies. But shortly afterwards the New River directors changed their minds and began
negotiations with a view to drawing up a boundary.[2] However,
over two years of bargaining were still needed before agreement was reached, during which time active competition continued. Not until September 1815 were the details settled.
The agreed boundary left the New River Company in possession of the entire City, together with Islington, Holloway and
Stoke Newington. This secured Whitechapel, Wapping,
Bethnal Green, Hackney, Homerton and Dalston to the East
London. The line ran southwards along Kingsland Road as far
as   Shoreditch,   then   turned   south-eastwards   along

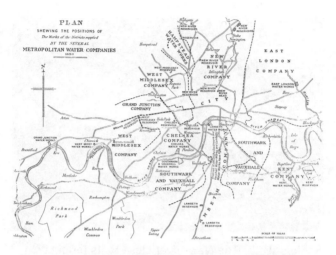

Map, 1850. This map is from the General Board of Health report of 1850; the boundaries north of the Thames are those of the 1817 General Arrangement.

Commercial Street, passing through the dock areas east of the Tower to the Thames. Counsel's opinion was taken as to whether a formal agreement between the companies could be made legal and binding, and as a result a Deed of Arrangement was drawn up and signed by the companies' Directors on 9 November 1815.[3]

   This deed not only fixed the boundary between the areas to be supplied but also included a covenant stipulating that supplying any houses in the other company's area would incur a penalty of double the water rates thus gained. Each company relinquished ownership of the pipes which it owned beyond its boundary: the New River pipes thus abandoned, which were wooden, were valued at £1,704, while the iron pipes given up by the East London were reckoned to be worth £8,855. The New River Company agreed to pay £700 per annum for ten years as compensation.[4] The New River gained former East London customers paying some £1,000 per year, and the East London gained over 3,700 extra houses paying more than £4,000 per year. The exchange of tenants was completed by April 1816.[5]

   The East London Company was very satisfied with its new

Sadlers Wells. The New River close to its termination at New River Head.

monopoly, the outcome of a few years' competition. In October 1816 the Engineer reported that an increase of a thousand tenants a year for the next ten years could be confidently expected, from the great numbers of houses being built in the company's exclusive area of supply, and in July 1817 he proposed that an additional steam engine should be erected at Old Ford and a new main laid to Whitechapel. The directors thought that 'however proper the adoption of such improvements might have been during Competition they could not with uncertain prospects have recommended the same. But in consequence of the Arrangement ... having given an immediate accession of Tenantry, the improving state of the Districts, the extreme low price of Iron and other materials including Labor, the great saving which will thereby be effected in the permanent expences, and lastly with a view of advancing the rates', the suggested measures could now be carried out. The consequent improvements in the service given to customers would, they felt, lead to the 'cheerful acquiescence' of the public in the proposed increased rates.[6] A new Boulton and Watt engine was duly ordered and erected in an additional engine house. The company's final verdict on the arrangement was given by the auditors' report to the General Assembly of Proprietors in October 1818. Remember, said the auditors, that 'from a variety of Causes, but principally from a ruinous competition with another company, not only was the Revenue so reduced, as if collected, not to be sufficient to pay a Dividend, but the collection itself was paralyzed by the operation of that competition ... the corner stone of the Company's prosperity was laid by the Arrangement with the New River Company.'[7]

While the East London Company's problems were solved by their agreement with the New River Company, the latter still faced vigorous competition from the West Middlesex, Grand Junction and York Buildings Companies, and was left as the only competitor of the moribund London Bridge Water Works. Early in 1815 the New River directors approached the West Middlesex Company, their most vigorous rival, with a view to reaching an agreement similar to that then being negotiated with the East London. Each company appointed a committee of directors, and the New River first suggested that a common schedule of rates should be agreed; the West Middlesex rejected this idea as it was using lower rates as the main means of gaining customers from its opponents. Then the New River proposed that the West Middlesex should agree to be bought out entirely, but this too was unacceptable. The New River committee's third proposal was for a boundary to be drawn up guaranteeing each company an exclusive area of supply, but the West Middlesex turned this down as well. The West Middlesex committee's preferred solution was for a 'complete and perfect Union of the two Concerns' to be brought about, and after months of haggling the details of such a union were finally worked out in August 1815. The capital of the New River Company was calculated to be £750,000 and that of the West Middlesex to be £350,000, the incomes from water rents being £68,000 and £10,000 respectively. The New River company estimated that £200,000 would have to be spent on 'turning wood into iron' in order to bring its existing mains network up to the standard of the West Middlesex. The New River Committee proposed a union on the basis of a 4:1 division of the combined profits, but the West Middlesex insisted on amending this to a 4:1 division for the first seven years and thereafter 4:1 for the first £600 per New River share and 2:1 for any profits above that. The board of directors was to consist of seven New River nominees and five West Middlesex. The public was to be protected 'against any effect from the Junction tending to a

Monopoly' by limits on either rates or dividends.[8] A special General Assembly of West Middlesex proprietors was called in September 1815 and approved the action taken by its committee.[9]

Active competition between the two companies ceased as soon as agreement had been reached, although an Act of Parliament would be needed to authorise their union, and both felt the benefits at once. As early as November 1815, the West Middlesex Engineer reported that 'the regularity of the supply gives universal satisfaction to the Public', and the directors recorded that the agreement had resulted in large arrears of rates being recovered which would otherwise have been lost. Over 400 houses had been added to the company's supply during the past six months, despite the cessation of attempts to gain tenants from the New River Company.[10] The West Middlesex Company confidently anticipated that the proposed union would guarantee future prosperity for its shareholders, as its Secretary assured one of them in October 1815.[11] The York Buildings Company evidently thought so too, for in February 1816 it applied to join the impending union, only to be rebuffed by the New River Company.[12]

The Bill to authorise the combination of the New River and West Middlesex Companies was introduced into Parliament early in the session of 1816. Great opposition was encountered from the other water companies, the vestries of parishes in the West Middlesex Company's district, and especially from the Grand Junction Canal Company, whose protégé the Grand Junction Water Works Company faced probable ruin if its two main competitors were allowed to combine. On realising the strength of the opposition, the two companies concerned withdrew the Bill to avoid fruitless expense.[13] The Grand Junction Directors reported this happy outcome to their shareholders in June 1816, commenting that the Bill would have enabled the West Middlesex Company to take over all the New River tenants in the West End, 'and prevented that loss of Tenants which the New River Company are almost daily suffering for want of a more efficient service'.[14]

Immediately after the abandonment of their Bill, the New River and West Middlesex Companies began further negotiations aimed at maintaining their independence while agreeing a boundary between their districts. In May 1816 the New River offered to give up its tenants in the area west of

Tottenham Court Road and north of Oxford Street in return for
the West Middlesex giving up its pipes east and south of this
line. The New River rental in the area to be handed over
amounted to £7,132 per annum, while the West Middlesex
rental for the area east of Tottenham Court Road was £2,618
(according to the New River Company) or £3,450 (according
to the West Middlesex Company), but the West Middlesex valued its pipes to be relinquished at £43,000, a figure which
the New River would not accept. No agreement could be
reached on this point, but the two companies did agree to
refrain from laying on supplies at reduced rates and from supplying or repairing tenants' lead pipes free of charge.[15] In
August 1816 the companies reached an outline agreement
that each would retire gradually within a mutually acceptable
boundary,[16] and by January 1817 negotiations had been concluded and a boundary fixed along the Tottenham Court
Road/Oxford Street line.[17]

By that time, complicated bargaining had been going on
among all the water companies with a view to reaching a 'general arrangement' to end the competition. The New River
Company's agreement with the East London had left the former opposed only by the London Bridge Water Works in the
eastern part of its area, and the contest between the two
proved to be very unequal. As Richard Till of the London
Bridge Works later put it, 'the New River have the power of
raising their water higher than we do; the manner in which
houses have been built within thirty years, have carried up
their cisterns and their water closets much higher, and from
that we are much injured ... We have no site to put a steam
engine on, the neighbours would not permit it.'[18] The New
River Company, on the other hand, was already (since 1812)
laying iron pipes, after an attempt to pump a high-pressure
supply through its wooden mains and services which resulted
in them becoming 'full of Leaks and Weeps',[19] and was now
able to offer supplies to the tops of houses. The London Bridge
managers, therefore, approached their powerful rival in March
1816 requesting 'an arrangement between the Collectors of
the two Companies in those parts of the City where their Pipes
come into contact so as to do away entirely the unpleasant
misunderstanding and Warfare which at present subsists to
the great detriment of both concerns'.[20] The New River
Company proved unreceptive, and the introduction into

Parliament of Michael Angelo Taylor's Metropolis Paving Bill, which would compel them to renew all their wooden pipes in iron, greatly alarmed the London Bridge managers. The Bill failed in the 1816 session but was renewed in 1817, and threatened to involve the London Bridge Works in a capital expenditure of about £60,000 which could not possibly be raised.[21] The managers petitioned the House of Lords against the offending clause of the Bill, and succeeded in amending it so that the Act as passed allowed wooden mains to be repaired and existing wooden pipes to be replaced with wood if desired, while all new mains must be iron. This was a great relief to the London Bridge managers.[22] By November 1817, however, the New River Company had laid iron pipes 'through every street in the City', and industriously canvassed every householder there, so that the London Bridge Works was rapidly losing tenants and its future looked very doubtful.[23]

The York Buildings Company, too, was in considerable difficulty by 1816. It had laid out £150,000 capital on a system of iron mains and services, but despite very active competition its annual income from water rents was only £3,730. The directors decided, after the failure of the New River/West Middlesex union which they had hoped to join, to give up the unequal struggle, and in May 1816 an agreement was concluded with the New River Company. The New River was to purchase a 96-year lease of all the York Buildings pipes and works in return for two down payments of £5,000 each and an annual payment of £2,250.[24] The arrangement was not finally signed until March 1818, and the York Buildings pipes were formally handed over on 25 November 1818, but the New River Company had been collecting the rents from York Buildings tenants since midsummer 1816.[25] The York Buildings Company had effectively ceased to exist as a water undertaking from that date, although the company lasted on until it was dissolved by Act of Parliament in 1829.[26] The final Act provided for a payment by the New River Company of £250.18s.6d. per annum to the York Buildings proprietors and their heirs, an obligation which was inherited by the Metropolitan Water Board in 1903.[27]

While the West Middlesex and New River Companies were negotiating their boundary, and the latter was taking over the York Buildings works, the Chelsea Company was approached to come into a 'general agreement'. In May 1816 it received a

letter from the West Middlesex proposing that 'some recipro-
cally beneficial Arrangement might be effected ... as to the
supply of Houses in those Districts where the Chelsea and
West Middlesex Companies were alone in competition'.[28] The
West Middlesex would give up its mains and services in
Walnut Tree Walk, Seymour Place, Fulham Road and sixteen
other streets, 'retiring wholly from Little Chelsea with their
pipes' and giving up an annual rental of £130. In return, the
Chelsea Company was asked to withdraw from Paddington
and Marylebone, where it possessed about five miles of wood-
en pipes worth £4,000.[29] The Chelsea Company acceded in
principle in July 1816, agreeing to 'a partial exchange of
District', exchanging 'the pipes value for value, and the Rent,
Rental for Rental', with any balance either way being made up
in cash. The West Middlesex was to give up its pipes south
and east of the Brompton Road, while 'The Chelsea Company
proposes ceding all their pipes and Rental in such parts of the
Parishes of Marylebone and Paddington, at the north of the
New Road and retiring from that District for Ever'.[30]

The Chelsea directors, while ready to cease opposing the
West Middlesex, considered intensifying their efforts against
the Grand Junction by laying iron mains in the parish of St
George Hanover Square and around Grosvenor Square; they
reluctantly decided, however, that the expense of £28,000
involved was beyond their means.[31] Instead, they negotiated
directly with the Grand Junction Company as well, and by
March 1817 a general settlement had been agreed among all
the companies concerned. The Chelsea directors recorded
that the present competition was 'particularly ruinous' to their
Company as a result of the 'insurmountable difficulties this
Company has to encounter in supplying the Upper District, so
as to be able to contend with those Companies who from their
local situation can *there* with ease afford a very superior and
also a much cheaper service',[32] and so they readily fell in with
an offer from the Grand Junction. This offer restricted the
Chelsea Company to a district comprising Chelsea proper,
Kensington, Westminster proper and areas between, and the
company would lose rents to an annual value of £5,285 from
its tenants outside the district; it would gain £1,478 per
annum from rents from present Grand Junction and West
Middlesex tenants inside its allotted district, and the directors
calculated that it would save £2,647 per annum in the

expense of maintaining its pipes.[33] They felt that 'in the event
of possessing the above District, independent of all other
Companies, a small Increase of Rent, perfectly consistent with
the Service, would more than compensate the loss
of £1,160'.[34]

On 3 July 1817 representatives of the New River, West
Middlesex, Grand Junction and Chelsea Companies met to
agree the final partition of the West End and the end of competition. The Chelsea Company secured a district approximately as had been agreed with the Grand Junction.[35] The
West Middlesex obtained confirmation of its agreement with
the New River Company and was to supply an area comprising St Pancras west of a line from Fig Lane along Hampstead
Road and Tottenham Court Road to Oxford Street, most of
Marylebone (including the new Regents Park), part of
Kensington and Hammersmith.[36] The Grand Junction's area
included Paddington, Bayswater and the part of Westminster
known as Mayfair: although relatively small, this would produce water rents amounting to some £12,600 per annum.[37]
The New River Company, although giving up the right to supply large areas in the West End, was confirmed in its possession of the City and such prosperous areas as Bloomsbury and
Holborn, while its impending purchase of the York Buildings
works would secure Soho. The companies were convinced of
the necessity for this General Arrangement. The West
Middlesex directors reported to their shareholders that the
only means by which the companies' losses could be ended
'without proving injurious to the public, was the concentration
of the respective works ... to prevent the sacrifice of Capital
required by the new Paving Act, in substituting Iron Pipes for
Wood'.[38] The Chelsea directors, on 16 October 1817,
'Resolved, That the Company do retire from such parts of their
present Service as are inconvenient and expensive to them ...
whenever the other Water Companies shall proceed therein.'[39]
Negotiations in respect of the sums owed for pipes relinquished by the Arrangement continued for some time, however, and it was not until July 1821 that the last exchange, of
239 yards of iron pipes belonging to the West Middlesex
Company and valued at £52 for 203 yards of pipes belonging
to the Chelsea Company and valued at £57.11s., was put
into effect.[40]

Although the General Arrangement seemed to the companies to be generally beneficial to all of them and also to the public, the agreements could not be openly arrived at or put into the form of binding covenants, as had the East London/New River Company agreement. The Grand Junction and West Middlesex Water Works Acts contained clauses prohibiting those companies from selling or assigning any of their rights of supply, so there were grave doubts as to whether the present agreements were legal.[41] For this reason, the public were given no inkling of the negotiations, and the unfortunate customers who were to change companies had no warning of that fact. At Christmas 1817, a large number of householders in the West End suddenly found themselves without a water supply, and some days later were presented with handbills informing them, with thanks for their support during the period of competition, that the company could no longer afford the expense of supplying the area and had therefore withdrawn. During January 1818 those householders were canvassed by other water companies, those which had been guaranteed the exclusive supply of the area. The contest was over.

Chapter 5
The question of charges
1818–1821

In the early nineteenth century the parish of St Marylebone
was administered by a Select Vestry which was among the
most influential in the country. Established by an Act of 1768,
the vestry had 122 members, of whom normally only thirty
were tradesmen, the rest being peers and gentlemen.[1] In
1819, the list of vestrymen included nine members of the
House of Lords and nine of the House of Commons.[2] The
parish itself had, during the course of the eighteenth century,
changed from a small village just outside London to one of the
wealthiest and most prosperous parishes in the metropolis,
and it was continuing to grow: its 1,499 acres held 63,982
people in 1801, 75,624 in 1811 and 96,040 in 1821.[3]
Much of the new building, including the elegant terraces of the
new Regents Park development which had transformed the
old Marylebone Park, was of the most fashionable kind. Such
a wealthy area demanded an efficient local government system, and by the standards of the time it got one. The streets of
Marylebone were better lit and more effectively watched than
most, the parish fire-fighting service was also above average,
and the regular paving of the parish's streets was the envy of
those slipping in the mire of nearby Westminster.[4]

Marylebone had been the scene of the fiercest competition
among the water companies between 1810 and 1817, with
first the West Middlesex and then the Grand Junction
Companies striving to oust the established Chelsea and New
River Companies: it was one of the few areas which had as
many as four companies competing for its custom. The large
number of good quality houses made the parish of particular

significance to companies hungry for water rents, and after the 'General Arrangement' the parish was to provide nearly the whole of the West Middlesex Company's income. The Grand Junction Company took only a small part of Marylebone, which nevertheless was expected to yield a significant portion of that company's revenues. The Select Vestry had previously clashed with the companies, firstly in 1809–10 when the West Middlesex Company sought power to enter the parish, and later during the competition period when the various companies were constantly breaking up the paved streets in order to lay pipes and connect new customers to the services.[5] In general, however, the vestry approved of the competition as it reduced the water rents and had induced the companies to water the streets free of charge.

The withdrawal of certain water companies from parts of their areas at the end of 1817 naturally created alarm and annoyance among their abandoned customers – particularly as there was a significant time-lag between the loss of the old supply and the provision of the new. John Thomas Hope, for example, who resided at 37 Upper Seymour Street and was a member of the Select Vestry, had a supply from the New River Company to his house and from the Chelsea Company to his coach-house. At Christmas 1817 he found that both companies had cut off the supplies, reducing his tenants who lodged above the coach-house 'to the necessity of going about begging for water wherever they could get it'. It was not until 18 January 1818 that the New River Company gave Mr Hope a notice that the supply had been cut off, and on 21 January he received a letter from the West Middlesex Company offering to supply him. He eventually applied to the latter company, but was then told that the letter had been sent to him in error and that he should apply to the Grand Junction Company. This he did, but it was not until midsummer 1818 that he again received a regular supply.[6] Many other customers were similarly treated, although some, such as John Richardson of Tichborne Street, were transferred from one company to another without even being aware of the fact until they received their next water rent demands.[7] Several areas of London were affected, but Marylebone suffered particularly severely: there the competition had been most intense and the various companies' areas were most intermixed.

The most vociferous protests at the end of the competition

period came from Marylebone, and particularly from the Select Vestry itself. On 17 January 1818 the vestry wrote to the four water companies concerned 'to inquire whether they are not withdrawing their supply of water from the parish of Mary-le-bone, or whether it is the intention of the companies to supply the inhabitants as heretofore, and at the same rates, or what the companies propose doing; in order that their answer may be laid before the parishioners who have expressed the greatest alarm and apprehension on this important and serious subject'.[8] The companies responded by suggesting that their representatives should meet with a committee of the vestry, and the meeting was held on 3 February. The West Middlesex deputation gave an assurance that their company was well able to give Marylebone a much better supply of water than it had previously enjoyed, but that it could not be expected to continue such an improved supply without raising charges to the levels which had applied before competition began. Although the West Middlesex and Grand Junction representatives stated that they did not intend to raise their charges immediately, they also said that such an increase would in due course be necessary, and that additional charges would be made for 'high service', over and above the old rates. The most the New River Company would concede to the vestry committee was that it would retain the physical power to re-enter the parish should this appear to be of advantage to the company in the future, and that an emergency service from the Tottenham Court Road main could be given in the event of serious fires or other calamities.

The vestry committee quickly grasped the realities of the position, and reported that 'the competition, which was the foundation of the West Middlesex and the Grand Junction companies application to Parliament for their acts, and which induced Parliament to grant them, is now completely done away, and the parish is not only deprived of that advantage, but is left exposed to all the uncertainty, and the numerous evils, such a situation subjects them to.' The committee indignantly pointed out that the many parishioners who were without water must apply to whichever company had arbitrarily taken control of their area, and must pay the cost of connecting their houses to that company's services. It was felt that the vestry must 'prevent, if it be possible, the parish being delivered over to the mercy and discretion of perpetually fluctuat-

ing boards, who may make such exorbitant demands, that will
materially deteriorate the property of this parish'. To this end,
the committee recommended that the vestry should consider
setting up a parochial water works, to be funded by a combination of loans and rates in the same way that £200,000 had
been raised and paid off for paving the streets. On 14
February 1818 the Vestry Board approved the committee's
report, and resolved to carry its recommendation into effect.[9]

The water companies soon learned of the vestry's resolution, and were extremely alarmed. This proposal threatened to
overthrow the whole basis of the 'General Arrangement',
which depended upon the West Middlesex Company's possession of the lion's share of Marylebone. A parochial water
works, even if not entirely successful, would effectively renew
the competition in Marylebone and probably ruin the West
Middlesex Company, while if the project were successful the
company's main assets, its mains and services throughout
Marylebone, would become valueless. All four companies
concerned agreed to oppose the vestry's application to
Parliament.[10] The support of George Byng, MP, who had been
of great assistance to the West Middlesex Company in 1810
was also enlisted.[11] The West Middlesex directors, in a state of
panic, rashly wrote to the vestry on 19 February promising
'that no advance will be made in the rates *until* the parishioners are indemnified for the expense they have incurred in
the change from the old works, nor will any advance whatever
be made for the usual supply of water, beyond what the inhabitants paid to the old companies in the year 1810.'[12] The company noted the resentment among the public at having to pay
a connection charge on being transferred from one company
to another, and resolved that in future such charges would be
waived. Those customers who had already paid the cost of
making good the paving disturbed in making connections
would be reimbursed.[13]

Despite these placatory efforts the vestry remained indig-
nant, and determined to proceed with its scheme for a
parochial water works. On 26 February the West Middlesex
directors learned that a vestryman, Sir James Graham, had
alleged that their activities since 1810 had involved the vestry
in expense amounting to £50,000 for repairing paving damaged during mainlaying. They promptly wrote pointing out
that the company had always reimbursed such expense.

Nevertheless, on the same day that the vestry received this letter, it resolved unanimously to apply to Parliament for power to construct its own water works, and also for power to contract with any water company for a supply to the parish, as an alternative.[14] The vestry then wrote to the New River, Chelsea, West Middlesex and Grand Junction Companies, requesting that their representatives attend a meeting on 4 March.

At that meeting the various companies put their points of view to the vestry committee. The New River stated that it had already lost large sums in supplying the parish during the competition period, and could not afford to maintain such a competition. It was satisfied that the West Middlesex and Grand Junction would deal fairly with the parishioners, but would undertake to negotiate to provide a supply 'if the companies in question make immoderate demands upon the parish'. 'But until it shall appear that the West Middlesex or Grand Junction companies refuse to treat upon moderate terms, and attempt to abuse their situation, the New River company decline to enter into such a treaty.' No definitions of 'moderate terms' or 'abuse' were given, so it appeared that the New River's undertaking was valueless. The Chelsea Company merely said that it had no proposals for supplying Marylebone, 'the company having already lost a considerable sum of money therein'. The Grand Junction gave its view that its portion of Marylebone could be served in return for an overall charge of £3,000 per annum, including high service. The West Middlesex, after taking two days to calculate its figures, wrote to the vestry on 6 March alleging that it had spent £250,000 on supplying Marylebone, that its annual expense in respect of supplying the parish amounted to £5,000, and that it considered an income of £17,500 per annum to be necessary in order to cover that expense and provide a fair return on capital. The directors estimated that return as 4% after allowing for 'extraordinary expenses'.[15]

The vestry, which detected a conspiracy aimed at extorting immoderate charges from the parish, was not at all satisfied with these answers, and demanded that the companies undertake to supply the parish at rates 10% below those of 1810. This demand appeared not unreasonable in view of the general fall in prices and wages since that date, but it took no account of the improved methods of supply which were now in use, at great expense to the companies. All the companies refused to undertake to supply the parish on these terms, and the West Middlesex moreover withdrew its rash promise not to advance beyond the 1810 water rates. The company now undertook only to 'investigate the existing rates, and equalize them on a just and reasonable scale, according to the nature and extent of the supplies required, in order that such a moderate advance only, as may be found absolutely just and necessary, may be determined'.[16] On 2 May 1818 the West Middlesex and Grand Junction Companies put their proposals for increasing their charges which were calculated as follows:

Rates charged in 1809		Rates charged in 1817	
New River	£11,182. 2s. 0d.	New River	£ 5,648. 3s. 6d.
Chelsea	£ 2,205.18s. 6d.	Chelsea	£ 1,177.12s. 6d.
Total	£13,388. 0s. 6d.	West Middlesex	£ 3,286.18s. 6d.
		Grand Junction	£ 871.10s. 0d.
		Total	£10,930. 4s. 6d.

The companies proposed to increase the rates for 'ordinary supply' to a level 25% above the 1809 rates, that is to a total of £16,735.0s.7½d., plus £2,500 to allow for houses now in supply which had not then existed, and additional charges for 'high service'. They pointed out that the parish now received far more water than previously (they estimated four times as much), and that the existence of iron mains, permanently charged, all over the parish afforded an unprecedented security against fire. 'In consequence of the abundant supply, superior attention, and accommodation now existing, the habits of the parishioners are naturally changed; so much so, that nothing short of a continuance of this supply and attention will now be satisfactory to them.' The companies submitted that they had 'a fair and irresistible claim for the before-mentioned advance, and which they hope will be readily allowed them'.[17]

Their hopes proved to be vain. The vestry immediately petitioned Parliament for leave to bring in its Bill, which was read a first time on 6 May.[18] The companies enlisted their parliamentary supporters, who now included Sir James Graham and Michael Angelo Taylor, to oppose it, and the latter agreed to introduce a Bill on behalf of the companies to give them statutory authority to fix charges. They also obtained petitions against the vestry's Bill signed by many parishioners who feared a great increase in the parish rates. The vestry's Bill failed to progress further in the 1818 session.

After the withdrawal of the Marylebone Select Vestry's Bill the ill-feeling against the water companies appeared to have subsided. In November 1818 the West Middlesex directors reported to their shareholders that the work of changing consumers' supplies in Marylebone to the company's pipes had been completed, and that the consumers appeared to be satisfied with the supply. In addition, 'the prompt and abundant supply of water, at several recent Fires has fully demonstrated the power of the Company to afford ample protection, and its disposition to apply that power, on any emergency, to the public benefit.'[19] The Grand Junction directors similarly reported in December 1818 that many fewer complaints were now being received from consumers.[20] In the summer of 1818 the two companies had given notice to their customers, by printed leaflets, that their charges were to be increased: the Grand Junction's leaflets said that the increased charges would be collected on Lady Day 1819, and the West Middlesex's stated that they would be collected at Christmas 1818.[21] When the companies started to collect the increased rates, early in 1819, many customers were startled and enraged to find that the increase was back-dated to the previous Michaelmas or midsummer, and that in many instances the new rate was very much more than the old. The companies had first calculated the water rent which was, or would have been, payable for each property in 1810, then increased that by 25%, then added charges for high service on top; the effect in some cases was to double or treble the amount that had been charged in 1817. Dr Robert Masters Kerrison of New Burlington Street, for instance, paid £2. 2s. per annum to the New River Company until 1813, then changed to the Grand Junction at £2; from Michaelmas 1818 his rate was increased to £6 16s. 6d., much of the increase being due to the charge for high service.[22] Mr William Harris, of Norton Street, paid 30s. to the New River Company in 1810 and subsequently had his rate reduced to 24s.; from Michaelmas 1818 the West Middlesex Company demanded 37s. a year.[23]

The first result of these increases was that the Select Vestry again applied to Parliament and brought in a new Bill for its parochial water works. The West Middlesex and Grand Junction proposed that they and the vestry should jointly pro-

Office of Chelsea Water-Works,

ABINGDON STREET, WESTMINSTER.

The DIRECTORS of the CHELSEA WATER-WORKS having for a long time served their tenants with Water at Rates insufficient to meet their increased and increasing Expences; and, being further called upon, by a late Act of Parliament, to substitute Iron for Wood Pipes, heretofore used by the Water Companies, a new and most heavy expense, which they cannot possibly sustain without the assistance of their tenants, they are compelled to make a general Increase of their Rents; and they are fully persuaded not an unreasonable one, when the quantity of Water consumed, and the great Convenience afforded, are taken into consideration:—they beg, therefore, to inform you, that the Rent you are to pay from Lady Day 1818, is £

By Order of the Court of Directors,

Secretary

Handbill 2 – Chelsea Company, 1818. Its monpoly secured, the Chelsea Company gives notice of increased charges. The tone of this handbill is in marked contrast to the one of 1811.

mote a Bill to limit any increases in charges to a level 25%
above the 1810 rates, but the vestry refused this offer and
persisted with its own scheme. The two companies then pre-
vailed on Michael Angelo Taylor to introduce a Bill into
Parliament on their behalf. This Bill sought to limit water
charges to 25% above the 1810 level, for the 'ordinary service', but would permit additional charges for 'high service'
and trade use.

The water companies again opposed the vestry's Bill in the
Commons, and it failed to gain a second reading. The companies' Bill, however, passed through the Commons without difficulty and was referred to the Lords. The vestry petitioned the
Lords, and its counsel delivered a bitter attack on the companies before the Lords Committee. He accused the companies
of having raised and expended far more capital than was really required for their primary purpose of supplying water: 'Joint
Stock Companies', he said, 'though excellent servants, are the
worst of all masters; and that if unfortunately they are allowed
to ... raise capitals infinitely beyond their wants, there will be
sure to succeed pompous establishments, and prodigal expenditure'.[24] The secretaries of the West Middlesex and Grand
Junction Companies were strongly pressed to give details of
the 'General Arrangement' among the companies, but stoutly
professed their inability to do so, maintaining that the negotiations had not been minuted. They also denied that the
arrangement excluded companies from one another's districts; it was merely a matter of convenience, they said, that
each company should serve only the areas nearest to
its works.[25]

Counsel for the vestry, however, was unconvinced, alleging
that the arrangement was 'as unquestionably a conspiracy as
ever was the subject of Indictment before a Court of Justice'.
He also pointed out that the rates charged by the New River
Company in 1810 had been the highest ever charged, having
been increased between 1805 and 1807 from an average of
two guineas per annum to an average of 50s. for properties in
Marylebone, and maintained that the companies could easily
afford to supply the parish at lower rates. In support of this
assertion he produced Peter Potter, an engineer who had been
engaged by the vestry to design its parochial water works.
Potter gave details to the committee of this plan for supplying
9,000 houses and 80,000 people with 720,000 gallons of

water per day, at a total cost of £107,105. 9s. 2d. The vestry proposed to pay for this by a 6d. rate producing £13,606 2s. 6d. a year for 18 years, then a 3d. rate thereafter to pay maintenance costs.[26] When Counsel for the Bill showed Potter's qualifications for designing water works to be nil, the vestry brought in Ralph Walker, previously Engineer to the West Middlesex and East London water companies, to support Potter; it was then pointed out that Walker had produced over-optimistic estimates for water works in the past. The final assertion made by the vestry was that the water companies had incurred unnecessary expense by indulging in wasteful competition, and were now seeking to recoup their losses by charging unjustifiably high rates.[27]

Opposition to the companies' Bill did not come only from the vestry. The Lords committee heard from various fire agents who asserted that less water was now available for fire-fighting than had been during the competition period, from disgruntled consumers whose charges had been increased and, significantly, from James Weale, a government office-holder, resident of Marylebone and hater of water companies. He based his opposition on allegations that the West Middlesex Company had been a speculative swindle from start to finish and that the present directors of that company were seeking parliamentary sanction for further plundering of the public. At the same time, the vestry stirred up agitation against the water companies, holding meetings, posting placards throughout the parish and even on church doors, and distributing handbills urging consumers not to pay increased water charges.[28] To its satisfaction the Lords committee eviscerated the companies' Bill. As returned to the Commons it restricted the high service charges, gave consumers a right of appeal to Quarter Sessions against any charges, and limited the ordinary charges to those of 1810. Michael Angelo Taylor withdrew the Bill on its return.[29]

The vestry followed up its success by once again seeking to introduce a Bill empowering it to construct a parochial water works. The companies meanwhile collected their increased charges from most of their customers, but although nine-tenths of the West Middlesex Company's customers had paid by midsummer 1819,[30] a violent agitation against the companies was renewed during the autumn. The leading spirit in this agitation was James Weale, who founded the Anti-Water

Monopoly Association in October 1819 and wrote many pamphlets attacking the companies. The vestry encouraged Weale's activities: according to the West Middlesex Company Secretary, 'papers were sent into every house in the parish, not only by the committee called the Anti Monopoly Association, but also the vestry in their collective capacity, papers signed by the vestry clerk by order of the vestry ... all of them calculated to excite the greatest discontent, most of them containing misrepresentations of fact, and inclosing papers identifying the vestry to a great extent with the proceedings of the association'. The company pointed out the great influence which the vestry had in the parish: 'these documents, in which the inhabitants generally were informed that they were paying an enormous rate that could not be legally justified, would make a very great impression on the parish ... coming as it did from ... the select vestry of the parish, composed of noblemen and gentlemen; and it is not to be wondered at that complaints of the increase began to be heard'.[31] Weale did not confine his activities to Marylebone, but distributed leaflets and held meetings in St George's Hanover Square, St Pancras, Paddington and St James's. The policy of members of the association was to refuse payment of increased charges, tendering instead the rates charged in 1817. Their avowed aim was to induce the companies to prosecute them for payment, thus establishing a legal precedent one way or the other, but the companies refused to oblige and instead cut off the water from the recalcitrant consumers. On 22 April 1820 William Freemantle MP, chairman of the association's general committee, wrote to the Grand Junction Company offering to recommend those customers whose supplies had been cut off to pay their charges in full, provided that the company would agree to refund any excess if a court decision subsequently fixed lower rates. The company replied with dignity that 'it could not in any way recognise this self-constituted body who acting in no corporate capacity and possessing no legal rights were incompetent to bind any individual for whom they assumed to act'.[32] Its view of the association was of 'A few individuals ... who seem to believe that they can compel the Company to afford a supply of Water to the Inhabitants at any price they themselves chuse to fix and who ... have by the circulation of inflammatory papers and hand Bills so poisoned the minds of many of the Inhabitants as to

John Bull's WATER WORKS! or Unfeeling Speculators threatening to cut off one of the Necessaries of LIFE!!

Cartoon, 1819. The baffled fury of the Anti-Water Monopoly Association, denied its day in court by the companies' policy of disconnection, is evident in the extreme vulgarity of this cartoon.

have induced them to with-hold the payment of the Rates.'[33]

The Association was most active in late 1819 and early 1820, but by the middle of 1820 it was losing support and the companies were benefiting by their assiduous efforts to explain their position by leaflets and personal visits to customers. The Grand Junction Company was able to record in June 1820 that 'the numbers of the company's opponents have been considerably diminished', its explanation to the public of the basis of charge having counteracted 'the false statements and wilful misrepresentations of certain persons'.[34] The company felt that the dispute could best be solved by a parliamentary committee investigating the question fully. The association, in an effort to bring about its own prosecution, applied for an injunction to prevent the companies cutting off supplies from its members, but the Lord Chancellor refused to grant this. By the end of 1820, in the view of the Grand Junction directors, its activities were 'becoming every day of less importance'.[35]

Similar agitation occurred elsewhere in London, although hardship suffered by the teeming poor of the East End naturally attracted less attention than did higher rates charged to the nobility and gentry of Marylebone. From the end of 1815 the East London Company had possessed an effective monopoly in its district by virtue of its agreement with the New River Company, and in 1817 increased its charges. The increase was based not on a percentage of the rates charged before competition began (in much of the district there had been no piped water supply previously) but on the principle of 'equalisation' – upwards. During the period of competition the company had been so eager to obtain tenants that it had accepted customers' own assessments of future demand when calculating charges, its main aim being to undercut the New River Company. Now it carried out a survey and found that many premises which had formerly been rated as private houses were in fact used for trade purposes, while many other houses were charged less than similar houses nearby. It therefore, evened out its charges, increasing its income from rates from £16,843 6s. 11d. in 1816 to £21,874 4s. in 1818.

Agitation similar to that in Marylebone followed: petitions were presented to Parliament by various groups of inhabitants. One, from the inhabitants of the Finsbury and Tower divisions of the City, alleged that they received a 'very insufficient supply of water', that Parliament's intention of promoting competition by authorising the East London Company had been defeated by the companies' combination, and that 'the charges already exorbitant were considerably increased'. Another, from various East End parishes, sought power to establish a new water company in order to overcome the evils of monopoly. The petitioners pointed out that 'a considerable proportion of the inhabitants are in indigent circumstances' and were unable to pay the 'exorbitant and increasing rates imposed upon them'. Both petitions laid stress on the dangers of fire, particularly great in an area where most houses were wooden, and complained that the East London Company was insufficiently attentive to this danger. Examples of individuals' water rates being increased by up to 400% were given. Both petitions also complained that the company cut off the supply to properties on which arrears were due, instead of prosecuting the defaulting tenant, so that the owner was forced to pay arrears before he could obtain a new tenant.[36]

The East London Company did its best to allay this discontent. Its chairman attended a public meeting in October 1818 which he 'addressed ... at considerable length, and was very

much interrupted', but the agitators would accept no compromise.[37] He was greeted at first with 'a profound and ambigu-
ous silence', then with 'universal and violent hissing'.[38] The
company then prepared a counter-petition to Parliament in
which its case was set out. It pointed out that capital of
£380,000 had been invested, on which a fair return was
sought. No increase in rates had been made until two years
after the agreement with the New River Company, and the
increases then made averaged only 25%. It denied the allegations made in the application for power to set up a new company, which 'abounds with the grossest misrepresentations ...
the Cases of fire are some of them untrue and the rest exag-
gerated and distorted'. The instances of enormous increases in
charges were individually dealt with: Mr. Talbot, for example,
complained that his rates had been increased from £4 to £16
per annum, but the company pointed out that 'he keeps a
receptacle for deranged persons consisting of several hundreds all requiring from the nature of their situation an abundant supply'. Mr. Nathan's rates had been increased from
50s. to £10 a year, but the Company had discovered that he
was a publican whose house was now on the main road from
the City to the docks, and that he charged for watering 'hundreds of cattle' there daily.[39] The company's case was successful, and the applications to Parliament were not
pursued.[40] There was no agitation against the New River
Company, which refrained from increasing its charges pending
the outcome of the complaints against the other companies.

The Anti-Water Monopoly Association appeared by the end
of 1820 to have reached an impasse. Many of its members
and supporters were now without piped water supplies, having refused to pay increased charges, and it had been unable
to provoke the companies into prosecuting them. It apparently decided that the best way of settling the matter
was to do what the Grand Junction Company had previously
suggested, to seek a parliamentary select committee to investigate the whole question of London's water supply. Early
in 1821, therefore, William Freemantle MP, a leading member
of the Association, moved for the appointment of such
a committee.[41]

Chapter 6
The Parliamentary Select
Committee of 1821

The Select Committee appointed by Parliament on 6 February
1821 was instructed to 'inquire into the past and present
state of the supply of Water to the Metropolis, and the Laws
relating thereto, and to report the same, together with their
observations thereupon, to the House'.[1] The appointment followed a brief debate in which the main speakers were William
Freemantle, one of the water companies' foremost opponents,
and Michael Angelo Taylor, a former critic of the companies
but now one of their supporters. Freemantle's involvement
with the Anti-Water Monopoly Association and Taylor's pro-
motion of the Metropolis Paving Act have been mentioned
above: Taylor, although MP for Durham, was prominent in
London affairs. His hostility to the water companies had arisen
from their too-frequent breaking up of paved streets to lay and
repair pipes, but had been overcome by the passage of his
own Act (which ensured that all new mains and services
would be iron rather than wood) and by the general reduction
in main-laying activities which followed the end of competition. When Freemantle spoke in the Commons of the water
companies having 'a monopoly, grievous beyond all former
precedent', Taylor, therefore, rose to defend them. He proposed that they should be allowed to fix their charges at a rate
25% above the present level, and, referring to his West
Middlesex Waterworks Bill of 1819, 'observed that since his
bill had been thrown out of the other house, a water fever had
raged through the metropolis, which it was impossible to
allay'. Taylor volunteered to serve on the committee, which
consisted of 27 Members and was chaired by Freemantle.[2]

The committee commenced hearing evidence on 16 February 1821 and continued until 30 March, sitting on three days each week. In all it heard 43 witnesses, of whom 20 were officers of the various water companies and one was chairman of the East London Company. Most of the others were opponents of the companies, including several members of the Anti-Water Monopoly Association, so the witnesses were more or less evenly divided between employees and critics of the companies. The great concern of the companies' witnesses was to show that the companies had acted fairly, that they had not sought to 'oppress the public' by levying unreasonably high charges, and that no undue profits had been made. They were incidentally anxious to show that the hostile witnesses were activated by motives of spite or were just wrong in their facts – but in view of the identity of the committee's chairman they had to be careful in this. The anti-company witnesses were mostly householders who considered that they had been overcharged or otherwise unfairly treated. A few, however, were acting out of a belief that the companies were more sinister, and controlled by men guilty of a conspiracy to defraud the public on a grand scale. Prominent among these was James Weale.

The committee began by calling a series of water companies' officers to establish the facts about the current state of London's water supply. These witnesses were closely examined and required to give figures of the number of houses supplied, the amount of water put into supply, and details of the machinery and other capital equipment used. Sometimes they showed embarrassing ignorance: William Chadwell Mylne, engineer to the New River Company, for instance, was unable to give figures of the amount of water supplied by his company. To the committee's incredulous question 'Do you mean to say that the company are ignorant of the quantity of water supplied from their works?' he could only answer 'They know nothing more than what the river produces'. Again, Mylne was asked how many houses were supplied by his company, and answered 'I cannot give it directly; 52,000 tenants were supplied since the year 1817, and they cannot have varied much'. The combined evidence of the engineers and secretaries of the companies, however, effectively showed that far more water was now supplied to most parts of London than had been before 1810, and that 'high service' was now much more common. The first six days were taken up by evidence from company witnesses, together with statements from officials of the Court of Sewers as to the extent to which the flow of water into the sewers had increased since 1810.

The committee's third week opened on 2 March with the redoubtable James Weale being called. Weale's evidence occupied the whole of the session of 2 March, and most of that of 5 March, and consisted largely of a diatribe against the companies in general. The West Middlesex Company was singled out for special opprobrium, but the other new companies were also abused with vigour and venom. Weale's target was the whole principle of having water, 'one of the elements necessary to existence, the same as light and air, and not merely an article of subsistence like corn', being supplied by joint-stock companies whose principal concern must always be their own profits rather than the welfare of the community. He considered that the supply of water should be 'profuse, rather than merely sufficient, and gratuitous to the poor'. 'The costs of the works required to provide the supply', Weale believed, 'and the expenses attending the delivery of it, should be defrayed out of a local revenue, in the same manner as the expenses of the pavements, drains, police &c are, raised by an equitable assessment on the property of the district; and the management of such an establishment should be placed in the hands of commissioners, under the like regulations as the commissioners of sewers'. Weale's thinking is thus shown to be ahead of his time: he aimed to place the water supply of London in the hands of a public body such as the later Metropolitan Water Board. He also gave closely reasoned arguments against allowing the present companies, if they were to continue in existence, any increase in charges above the levels of 1810. He quoted at length from the publicity material distributed by the West Middlesex and Grand Junction Companies in their early days, promising abundant water at high pressure and low cost, and argued that they should now be compelled to perform as they had promised.

Weale was followed by a series of witnesses who complained of excessive charges and the committee recalled officers of the companies concerned to answer the complaints. Shirley David Beare, for example, a partner of Mr. Hatchett, a hotel-keeper in Piccadilly, testified that until 1814 they had paid a total of £11 4s. in water charges, £9. 2s. to the

Chelsea Company and two guineas to the New River. The Grand Junction Company had then solicited their custom, offering to supply the hotel for £6 per annum, and stating that as the supply would be constant, Mr. Hatchett 'might confidently do away with many cisterns which were then necessary as reservoirs from the two former companies'. From late 1818, however, the supply became intermittent as well as 'scanty', and in 1820 the charges were increased to 25 guineas per annum, the increase being back-dated to Michaelmas 1818. William Anderson, engineer of the Grand Junction Company, explained that the Company had employed one of the waiters in the hotel as a spy to ascertain the amount of water used, and had based the increased charge on the number of times the water-closets were flushed. He attributed the inconvenience suffered by the hotel when the supply became intermittent to a lack of proper cisterns, and justified the increased charges by pointing out that the Pulteney Hotel and the Duke of Wellington each paid £25 a year. It became evident that Beare's recollection of events and conversations differed from Anderson's, and such discrepancies between customers' and officers' statements were apparent throughout the evidence. It did emerge from this case, however, that the Grand Junction Company had, in 1818, suddenly and without notice ceased the constant supply which had previously been its major advantage over its rivals and adopted their intermittent system.

The committee, having heard a great number of complaints and the companies' answers, went on to examine the financial bases of the companies. Statements were taken from the company secretaries as to the amount of capital raised and expended and the fluctuations of share prices, and calculations made as to running expenses and profits. M.K. Knight, the secretary of the West Middlesex Company, was subjected to particularly searching questioning in view of Weale's allegations against his company's proprietors, and was able to satisfy the committee that there had been no impropriety in the financing of the company.

Having taken the evidence, the committee then spent six weeks drawing up its report, which was presented to the House of Commons on 18 May 1821. The committee found that each of the 'old' water companies, namely the London Bridge, New River and Chelsea, had each possessed an effective monopoly in its own district, and that these monopolies had been overthrown by the establishment of the East London, West Middlesex and Grand Junction Companies. 'The principle of the acts under which these companies were instituted was to encourage competition; and certainly in this as in other cases, it is only from competition ... that a perfect security can be had for good supply.' Nevertheless, 'from the peculiar nature of these undertakings, the principle of competition requires to be guarded by particular checks and limits in its application to them, in order to render it effectual without the risk of destruction to the competing parties, and thereby ultimately of a serious injury to the public.' The committee thus recognised that the capital assets of water companies consisted of their pipes and machinery which were merely the means of delivery for a commodity in itself of no market value, making the companies capital-intensive. In these circumstances, where a genuine competition was carried on it could be only at the cost of failing to obtain any reasonable return on the large capital invested, and would eventually result in ruin. The 'General Arrangement' among the companies and the buying-out of the York Buildings and London Bridge Works, then, 'carrying with them so much appearance of a combination against the public', appeared to have been 'measures of self-preservation'. The committee was, therefore, satisfied that the alarm and agitation which had been excited against the companies from early 1818 onwards was unjustified, even though understandable.

The committee went on to consider the question of the reasonableness or otherwise of the companies' charges. Firstly, they stated that the supply of water to London had undoubtedly improved in respect of quantity, regularity and reliability, 'with the further benefit that the security against fire is increased, and that by the establishment of communications between their works, the powers of the companies may be brought in aid of each other, in case of emergency'. They were of the opinion that 'the present supply of water to London is very superior to that enjoyed by any other city in Europe' - high praise for the companies. However, the report went on to consider the allegations that the new companies had expended capital far more prodigally than had been necessary, and were now seeking to obtain a return on that excessive capital by levying exorbitant charges. The committee did not feel themselves competent to judge whether the new companies' works might have been constructed more cheaply; 'it could not be safely decided, so as to justify an interference of the Legislature affecting private property, without the assistance of very skilful and experienced engineers, unconnected with the parties concerned, and having the opportunity of an actual survey ... to guide their judgements'. Nevertheless, on the basis of the figures given to them, they did not agree with the companies' critics that the old levels of charges would give an adequate return. They were, however, disturbed by the untrammelled power which each company possessed to fix its own level of charges, although they recognised that 'though the experiment of competition ... has failed, the present situation of the companies is such, that a considerable practical check against abuse ... may be expected from the apprehension of its renewal'. They, therefore, proposed that a Bill should be introduced into Parliament to fix the maximum charges for water supply at a level 25% above that of 1810 for the 'ordinary service', 'leaving high and extra services as matters of agreement between the parties, but defining the one and the other'. The Bill should be limited to four years, and the whole question reconsidered at the end of that time after careful examination of the companies' books.

The findings of the committee were, therefore, generally favourable to the companies, even though the chairman had been one of their leading opponents. In the event, although Freemantle did introduce a Bill to regulate charges for the next four years, it failed to obtain a second reading.[3] The companies remained within their agreed boundaries, although expanding their districts to keep pace with the outward growth of London, and retained the power to fix their own levels of charges. Several other Parliamentary Committees and Royal Commissions inquired into the water supply of London over the next thirty years, but no general Act was imposed on the companies until the Metropolis Water Act of 1852 – and that Act, being concerned mainly with water quality, did not even mention the level of charges.

Chapter 7
Fraud and investment: the men behind the companies

The projectors and proprietors of the new water companies were not, by and large, men who have left a mark on history. They must have been men of substance to have bought £100 shares, even by instalments as was the usual method, but they seem to have been mainly London-based merchants and tradesmen rather than landed gentry or 'gentlemen of fortune'. Of the 137 proprietors of the West Middlesex Company who received its first dividend in 1810, 90 can be identified with reasonable certainty: only 14 of these are accorded the title 'Esquire' by the London and Court directories. They included one peer, one peer's son and four naval officers, but no fewer than 70 were tradesmen of various kinds, among them merchants, lawyers, chemists, linen-drapers, weavers, dyers and the truss-maker to the New Rupture Society. They were no doubt prominent in their own world of business, but they were not men in public life and it is, therefore, difficult to identify their interests and analyse their motives. In a few cases, however, we know a little more than the names, addresses and professions of these people.

Perhaps the most important single individual in this episode was Ralph Dodd, the north country engineer who was instrumental in founding the South London, West Middlesex and East London Companies. His early career and activities up to his dismissal from his posts as Engineer to two of those companies have been mentioned in Chapter 2. Dodd's claim to notice rests on his having seen the possibilities for companies located on the outskirts of London and supplying water to the growing suburbs and semi-rural areas beyond the city, a

vision which he published in 1805.[1] Despite his lack of experience with water works, his practical involvement up to that
date having been with canals, all the companies which he
projected were actually established and indeed lasted for a
century, eventually supplying water to far larger areas and on a
much greater scale than he could have imagined; but he had
no part in their long-term success. He was dismissed by the
South London's directors in August 1805, a bare month after
the company's Act had passed, and by the East London
Company in August 1807, even before that Company's Act
had become law. The West Middlesex Company's original
Engineer, his son Barrodale Robert Dodd,[2] received the same
treatment from the directors, who picked a quarrel with him
and dismissed him in November 1806. Thus, only two years
after the publication of the schemes for new water works,
three companies had been established, but all three had
expelled the Dodds.

At the same time as Ralph Dodd was founding new water
companies in London, he was also active in promoting the
construction of bridges over the Thames, with the same lack
of personal success. In 1806 he was engaged as engineer on
the Vauxhall Bridge project, but was dismissed from this position in 1809, being eventually replaced by his rival John
Rennie. Dodd also projected water works in Kent (1809,
based in the Deptford/Greenwich area), Birmingham,
Colchester and Manchester and Salford, but by 1810,
although the companies were progressing, he had been
squeezed out of all of them. Clearly, either his ambitions and
ideas were not matched by his abilities as an engineer, or he
had some character defect which made him difficult to work
with. Support for the latter surmise is found in a report of a
hearing at Chelmsford Assizes in 1810, when Dodd was con-
victed of assault on the clerk to the Colchester Water Works
Company. He had formerly been employed as Engineer by the
company's directors, 'but for very good reasons they thought
it proper to dismiss him'. The assault occurred when the clerk
refused to let the ex-Engineer have the key to the works.
Dodd's Counsel said that he was 'an irritable man'; no doubt
by 1810 he had reason to be irritable with water companies.[3]

Earlier, in 1808, an information had been laid against him
in respect of his proceedings in projecting various joint stock
companies, it being alleged that he had acted in breach of the

'Bubble Act' of 1720 in raising capital without first obtaining parliamentary authority. The case was heard in the Court of King's Bench in May 1808, and excited public interest as being the first prosecution under the Bubble Act for 88 years. Lord Ellenborough gave judgement in Dodd's favour because the Act had been generally disregarded ever since 1720, and because 'it is a prosecution instituted by a person not injured or defrauded, the immediate object of the Statute being the protection of the unwary'.[4] Nevertheless, despite the failure of the prosecution Dodd had clearly broken the Act, and the fact that the case was brought indicates that some at least considered him dishonest rather than merely incompetent. Before this, in September 1807, the East London Company's directors thought it necessary to advertise in the London Gazette that Ralph Walker was now the company's Engineer and Ralph Dodd had no connection with the concern,[5] and Robert Buck, soliciting employment with the company in October 1807, stressed that he had no connection with Dodd. Buck felt that he should make the point because 'such a Character would tarnish that of any other person who might be considered to coincide with him'.[6] As early as 1802, before he had any connection with water works companies, Dodd had been dismissed from his position as an engineer on the Grand Surrey Canal.[7] Unfortunately, the reasons for Dodd's many dismissals are never specified, but he can scarcely have been either a capable engineer or a trustworthy financier.

After his sad experiences between 1805 and 1810, Dodd gave up water works companies, turning instead to bridges and steam engines. He had patented a fire-proof bridge in 1808, and worked with George Stephenson in patenting a steam locomotive in 1815. From 1814 he pioneered steam-boats, and his death in 1822 followed an accident in which the boiler of a steamboat burst. His activities cannot have been profitable, for he died in poverty.[8] Of his sons who had worked with him, George died of drink in 1827, while Barrodale Robert lived on until 1837 without achieving anything. Ralph Dodd's career was rather spitefully summed up in 1815 by his far more successful rival, John Rennie: 'With respect to Mr. Dodd ... I do not know a work he has successfully executed, but I know several in which he has completely failed.'[9] To the editor of the *Mechanic's Magazine* (1828), Dodd was 'a very ingenious schemer without any practical talent whatever';[10] but if he had no practical talent it is surprising that he was able to find employment with successive companies and in different engineering fields. His claim to fame is undoubtedly his initiation of a new style of water company: his shortcomings were apparently many and serious, but he left flourishing water companies in London and other parts of the country as his memorial.

A very different character was George Boulton Mainwaring, son of William Mainwaring, Tory MP for Middlesex from 1784 to 1802 (described by George Rudé as 'the corrupt old manipulator of the local bench'[11]). George Mainwaring defeated Sir Francis Burdett by five votes in the famous Middlesex election of 1804, and in 1806 his help was requested by the projectors of the East London Water Works Company in piloting their Bill through Parliament.[12] Although he lost his seat in October 1806, and was, therefore, unable to be of much assistance, he took a very active part in setting up the company and indeed took the chair at the first meeting of the directors in August 1807.[13] William Mainwaring acted as treasurer.

Under its Act of 1807, the East London Company was empowered to raise £100,000 in £100 shares, with the proviso that no individual was to hold more than 20 shares. By the end of 1807, although all shares had been taken, only £15,000 had actually been paid as instalments. In December 1807 it became apparent that considerably more capital would be required if the company were to purchase the West Ham and Shadwell works from the London Dock Company; Ralph Walker, the Engineer, valued those works at £60,000. The leading role in negotiating with the London Dock Company was taken by George Boulton Mainwaring, who on 15 December informed the directors that the asking price was £130,000, that the vendors would not reduce that price at all, and that a definite answer was required by 17 December.[14] The directors were 'greatly surpriz'd and disheartened by the enormity of the sum'; they felt that the proprietors would not agree to take on the responsibility for as many new shares as would be needed. There were 120 proprietors at the time, so each would be called upon to subscribe £1,000 on average, over and above the calls to which they were already committed. The possibility of extending the body of proprietors by making shares generally available to the public does not seem to have been considered. On 17 December, Mainwaring informed the directors that 'he had applied to several most opulent and respectable friends of his', and these had agreed to take on the responsibility for 400 shares, 'under the express condition that such shares should not be disposed of to prevent any depreciation in the value of such shares'. This meant that Mainwaring's friends agreed to subscribe £40,000, and the directors, relieved, decided that they would take 300 more of the new shares, leaving 600 to be divided among the proprietors at large. It was regarded as particularly important that shares should not be sold on the open market, since such sales could well lead to share prices being manipulated by speculators, resulting in unrealistic increases in value being followed by collapse – the 'bubble' effect.

The directors' proceedings were reported to a general assembly of the proprietors on 7 January 1808. It quickly became apparent that the proprietors, far from being unwilling to take on responsibility for more shares, suspected the directors of trying to secure an undue proportion of the expected vast profits of the company by reserving so many of the new shares to themselves.[15] The assembly did not approve the reservation of 300 shares to the directors, and would have disallowed the allocation of 400 to Mainwaring and his friends had he not pleaded that 'he had entered into an absolute promise and pledge to his said friends that such 400 shares should be so appropriated to them and that his honor and character were pledged to them'. He also pointed out that 'the opulence and weight of his said friends would make their Patronage and support as Proprietors very desirable to the Company, and that the Honor and propriety of their character would secure the performance of the said Condition not to sell the shares'.[16] The assembly then decided to permit the arrangement, so Mainwaring was allotted 400 shares and the remainder were divided equally among the proprietors. At its next meeting on 8 April 1808, the directors were commended for their 'very able and judicious management', and Mainwaring for his 'very able, upright and impartial conduct'.[17] The company duly obtained its second Act, empowering it to raise £130,000 in £100 shares and raising the limit on individual share holdings from 20 to 50.

During the next few months, disquieting reports reached the directors from the secretary that some of the shares allocated to Mainwaring and his friends had in fact been transferred to outsiders, and at a considerable premium. The deposits on the shares had been paid in the names of Samuel Gurney, Thomas Richardson, William Prescott, George Grote, John Masterman, Daniel Mildred and William Hubbard; Hubbard was an 'opulent merchant' and all the others were rich and well-known bankers, so the directors were very surprised that they should have found it necessary to dispose of their shares. In June 1808 the directors conveyed their 'disapprobation' to Mainwaring, but shortly afterwards fifteen of Masterman's shares were transferred. The directors' disquiet increased, as they knew Masterman to be very rich and respectable: he 'could not need the money, and would not deceive'.[18] They decided to investigate the relationship between Mainwaring and his alleged friends. One of the proprietors, Joseph Pattison, called on the bankers and found that none of them considered himself to be a proprietor of the company. Gurney, Richardson, Mildred and Masterman had agreed to have shares registered in their names but only as a convenience to Hubbard, who remained the owner, while Prescott and Grote knew nothing of the transaction at all. It became apparent that the arrangement set up by Mainwaring, with Hubbard's connivance, was a subterfuge intended to evade the statutory restriction on shareholdings.

The matter was reported to a general assembly of proprietors on 6 October 1808, by which time 181 of the 400 shares had been resold at premiums of between £50 and 70 guineas per share, a profit of between £10,000 and £12,000 'which may be fairly presumed to have passed through the hands of the said George Boulton Mainwaring and William Hubbard or one of them'. The bankers were exonerated of all blame, as being unaware of the purpose behind Hubbard's request for the use of their names; they had evidently been imposed upon by Mainwaring and Hubbard. The assembly resolved to take action in equity for the recovery of the shares improperly allocated and the profits improperly made. Mainwaring and Hubbard were to be allowed to retain only the 50 shares each which each had registered in their own names.[19]

George and William Mainwaring resigned from their positions as director and treasurer respectively of the East London Company in November 1808. At the next general assembly of proprietors, on 17 November, it was reported by the directors that Hubbard and Mainwaring had attempted to dispose of still more shares but that the company had refused to register the transfers. Counsel's opinion had been obtained, to the effect that 'the mode by which the appropriation of the 400 shares was obtained was a gross fraud on the Company and the said George Boulton Mainwaring and William Hubbard will not be suffered to retain any benefits from the transaction'. The bankers, however, 'have been deceived and imposed upon ... and thereby induced to lend their names ... they have been perfectly innocent of the least dishonourable Intention'.[20]

The company's suit against Hubbard, Mainwaring and four of the bankers (those who still retained shares registered in their names) was heard by the Lord Chancellor on 20–21 March 1809. Counsel for the plaintiffs put the company's case with some vigour, and Mainwaring then replied, alleging that he had acted throughout in the best interests of the company. He denied that he had undertaken not to re-sell any of the shares taken by himself and his 'friends', whom he knew only through Hubbard, not personally. He asserted that in December 1807 the high price demanded by the London Dock Company had so depressed him about the East London Company's prospects that he had sold five of his shares. It had appeared to him that the only way of placing the company on a sound basis was to obtain rich backers, and on meeting Hubbard on 16 December he had asked him to take on the responsibility for 350 shares. Later, in January 1808, he had asked Hubbard for the names of six wealthy friends in whose names 50 shares apiece could be registered. Hubbard's answer to the company's suit was a frank admission that he had taken 350 of the 400 shares, 50 in his own name and 300 held 'in trust for him' by the bankers. He had initially been unaware of the statutory limitation on individual share-holdings, and of the restriction on re-selling shares imposed by the company. He had made a profit of about £8,500 by re-selling the shares, and thought that he was entitled to retain this. The Lord Chancellor, however, ruled that the six bankers were not bona fide proprietors, and that Hubbard and Mainwaring were thus not entitled to more than 50 shares each. He gave judgement in the company's favour, Hubbard being ordered to repay £8,564. 8s. 4d. and Mainwaring to repay £550. The bankers were to restore their remaining

shares to the company. Hubbard, Mainwaring and the company were each to bear their own costs.[21]

Mainwaring appears to have been the leading light in this
attempted fraud, even though Hubbard made vastly greater
profits: during the hearing it was suggested that Hubbard had
agreed to make some of his profits over to Mainwaring, but
this was denied by both. In the event, both of them made not
inconsiderable profits out of selling the 50 shares each which
they were allowed to have, so all was not in vain from their
standpoint. Mainwaring was certainly not disenchanted with
water companies, for in 1811 he reappeared as one of the
original directors of the Grand Junction Water Works
Company, only to be compelled to resign in 1812 because of
his association with the Stone Pipe Company.[22]

One of the leading supporters of George Boulton
Mainwaring at the crucial general assembly of 7 January
1808 was Thomas Lumley, a merchant of Gutter Lane in the
City, who described Mainwaring as 'the Corner Stone of the
said Undertaking'.[23] Lumley was an active proprietor and promoter of the East London and West Middlesex Companies,
being a director of both and, from 1809, chairman of the latter. Equally prominent in both companies was George Watts,
a chemist in the Strand, who had led the agitation in the East
London Company against Mainwaring. Mainwaring, indeed,
told the Lord Chancellor that Watts had tried to buy some of
the 400 disputed shares from him at an early stage, and that
his refusal to sell was 'the cause of the dissatisfaction which
the said George Watts hath since affected and pretended on
the subject of this Defendant's Conduct'.[24]

In November 1809 Lumley and Watts were on a committee of West Middlesex Company directors negotiating for the
purchase of the York Buildings water works.[25] The asking price
was £26,000, and as the West Middlesex offer was increased
only to £22,000 the negotiations failed. Almost a year later, in
November 1810, it emerged that a group of West Middlesex
directors, including Lumley, Watts and two other members of
the negotiating committee, had purchased the York Buildings
works and were actively engaged in expanding its operations.
This came out at the meeting of proprietors on 6 November,
when Lumley complained that 'the Character of himself and
some of his Colleagues in the York Buildings Water Works,
also Directors of this Company, had been aspersed out of

Doors in consequence of his and their purchase of the York Buildings Water Works'. He asserted that the West Middlesex Company could not have effected the purchase without an Act of Parliament (although this had not been mentioned a year before). The meeting seemed to find it highly suspicious that the company's committee should have put through the purchase on their own account on the very next day after declining on cost grounds to buy on the company's behalf. Although another proprietor, George Clay, proposed a motion that it was highly desirable for the two companies to have directors in common in order to co-ordinate their activities, an amendment was put that no director of the West Middlesex Company should also be a director of a competing concern, and that the appointments of Lumley and his colleagues as directors should cease forthwith. This amendment was declared carried on a show of hands, but a ballot was demanded, which defeated the amendment by 142 votes to 120.[26] Lumley and his friends were thus saved from ignominious dismissal, but they had clearly lost the confidence of many of the proprietors.

Lumley, Watts and five other directors (more than half the Board) resigned with effect from 10 December 1810. Immediately afterwards, Lumley wrote to the West Middlesex Company proposing a friendly arrangement concerning areas of supply, but on 3 January 1811 the new directors resolved that 'no treaty' should be made with the York Buildings Company. They then demanded that the latter should entirely exclude itself from the area supplied by the West Middlesex Company, but this was refused.[27]

Lumley's departure from the direction of the East London Company was under a similar cloud: in April 1810 he resigned, with another director, due to 'aspersions' cast on his conduct by a general assembly of the proprietors. Unfortunately these aspersions were not minuted so we do not know their nature, but they were probably due to the extreme fluctuations in share prices.[28] The evidence for this is to be found in the report of the company's audit committee in 1812, which 'endeavoured to trace the excessive elevation that took place while the Works were yet unfinished, and the depression that followed after their completion'. The 'prodigious rise', thought the auditors, was due to 'the very injudicious and rapid increase of Shares and the mode of appropriation recommended by the Directors', assisted by the practice of declaring dividends out of capital at a time when no net profits had been made. The auditors were disturbed to find that 'the whole of the Directors who have retired from that situation, with one single exception, have secured to themselves and families very large sums of Money by the sale of their Shares and Appropriations', and had, therefore, sought legal opinion as to whether these former directors could be prosecuted. Although no such legal action was thought practicable, the conduct of the former directors was condemned, and the present directors were required to prepare full half-yearly accounts and submit them to auditors, in order to avoid any repetition of that questionable conduct.[29] It seems clear from this that Lumley and his friends were suspected of being speculators whose main interest in the company was to make quick profits by re-selling shares.

The group of West Middlesex Company directors who took over the York Buildings Water Works in late 1809 spent the next few years in raising £150,000 capital and expending it in efforts to compete with the other water companies, including the West Middlesex. As noted in Chapter 4, these attempts ended in complete failure, with the works being bought out by the New River Company. Lumley and his associates had expected to make large profits out of increased rental, but these hopes were not realised: 'they never received a dividend out of any profit whatever: from 1810 they paid two dividends, of £1 a share each, but it was out of the capital'.[30] This last proceeding, paying dividends out of capital in order to give possible investors a false idea of the company's profitability, had previously been carried out by the same men in the East London and West Middlesex Companies. Lumley apparently did not make any long-term profit out of his involvement with water companies, for he was declared bankrupt in 1813.[31] Presumably, any profit which he made out of share dealings with the West Middlesex and East London Companies was sunk in the York Buildings works.

George Boulton Mainwaring, Thomas Lumley and their friends seem to have been speculators rather than bona fide company projectors. Suspicions about the motives of many of the early directors of the East London and West Middlesex Companies were voiced at the time, and were vigorously revived in 1819 by James Weale of the Anti-Water Monopoly Association. Speaking before the Lords Committee considering

the West Middlesex and Grand Junction Water Works Bill, he
alleged that 'several of the original subscribers to these works
advanced their money ... from a deliberate design to make the
undertaking ... a means subservient to their dishonest
schemes for plundering unwary and credulous persons'.
Referring particularly to the West Middlesex Company, he said
that 'many of the original subscribers, who had promoted this
scandalous fraud ... sold their shares and retired from the concern', whereupon share prices collapsed.[32] Weale's allegations
are borne out by the West Middlesex and East London
Companies' share price fluctuations in 1809–11, the accusations made against Lumley and his associates in 1810, and
the East London Company auditors' report in 1812 (of which
Weale was probably unaware). The allegations were not
answered in 1819, but when Weale repeated them before the
1821 Parliamentary Select Committee he did provoke a
response. This time he described the original projectors of the
West Middlesex Company as 'a set of city speculators', and
compared the undertaking to Law's Mississippi scheme, on
which he had written a book.[33] The new companies were set
up, he alleged, 'without any permanent regard to the public
benefit, but merely to promote ... speculation in the shares of
the companies; that they look to profit from increasing the
market-price of the shares which they possessed, and realiz-
ing the premiums which they could obtain upon a transfer of
those shares'.[34]

The reply to these accusations came from M.K. Knight,
secretary of the West Middlesex Company, who maintained
that 'a more unfounded assertion was never thrown on any
man or body of men'. He pointed out that in 1812 shares in
the company were held by 224 individuals, of whom only 84
had since sold out, some at a considerable loss, while 210
proprietors had since bought in. Knight had examined the
share transfers between April and June 1810, the period of
sharpest rise in price, and found that only three individuals
had bought low and sold high, none of them having any connection with the direction of the concern. Knight took this as
conclusive evidence that Weale's allegations were unfounded.[35] He omitted to mention, however, that some of the original proprietors, who had bought at par, had sold their shares
at a premium in 1810; among these was Thomas Lumley,
who sold three shares at £50 premium in August, five at £20

premium in November and five at £12 premium in December. At that time premiums were falling and the company was discouraging sales as being likely to depress share values further, so Lumley's action is surprising if he had the best interests of the company at heart.[36] Knight himself, indeed, had appeared less convinced of the directors' innocence when he wrote to a proprietor in 1815 of 'the system of Delusion which, unfortunately for many, was practised by some of the Parties who had the conduct of this Undertaking'.[37] He can only have meant Lumley and his friends.

Some of the leading spirits in the new water companies, then, were probably speculators whose main concern was to make quick profits, although in Lumley's case it seems that he later lost those profits in another water company. The ordinary investor makes no such dramatic appearances in the records: his complaints at general assemblies of proprietors are briefly referred to or glossed over in the minutes, and any correspondence he had with the companies has generally not survived. Perhaps more typical than men such as Lumley, Mainwaring and Watts was William Ford of Edinburgh, who in 1810 bought five £100 shares in the West Middlesex Company, and in 1815 wrote to the company secretary to enquire why he had had no return on his investment. M.K. Knight's reply was a masterpiece; perhaps the letter owes its preservation to his satisfaction with it. He explained that Ford, far from being entitled to any dividend, should forfeit £60 which he had paid as instalments on a sixth share because he had been tardy in paying the balance of £40. However, Knight undertook to persuade the directors not to insist on forfeiture in this case, provided that the £40 was now promptly paid. He was also pleased to inform Ford that as new nominal £100 shares were being issued to existing shareholders for only £30 each, Ford's new investment would entitle him to three of these shares – the odd £10 would have to be written off.[38] The gullible Ford paid not only the £40 but also an additional £20 which entitled him to a fourth new share, but evidently required some further explanation, for Knight wrote to him again a month later, urging him to buy still more shares. 'The only way of retrieving your property, now, is to take as many Shares at the reduced price as you may obtain.'[39]

A month later still, Knight wrote again, explaining: 'The Capital expended in this concern being upwards of

£350,000, the Difference between the Shares at par and the present value (£30) has been lost by somebody. As matters at present stand you are one of the Losers ... According to my Calculation you ought to possess at least 19 Shares to reimburse the loss on the first or high-priced Shares: I do not hesitate, therefore, to recommend you to subscribe for the 10 Shares you Propose.' He ingeniously explained the benefits of buying even more: 'divide the capital, say £360,000 ... by 7,400 – the total Number of Shares raised and to be raised, it shows the average value of each Share to be about £40. If you take as many of the new Shares as will reduce the average price of your Shares to that sum, you cannot lose. All below that will be profit'.[40] There is no record of whether Ford actually did buy more shares, but if he did he no doubt regretted it, for no dividends were paid by the company until October 1819, and that was only 15s. per share.

These were the men behind the new water companies. They seem to have consisted mainly of well-to-do merchants and tradesmen with a few hundreds to invest, looking for a long-term investment which would show a steady dividend, but they undoubtedly included a minority of 'get-rich-quick' speculators whose involvement in the companies' early days intensified, if it did not cause, the tremendous fluctuation in share values. M.K. Knight may be permitted a sardonic comment on their activities, in conclusion. In 1814, writing to a proprietor who had missed the General Assembly, he said: 'There was little Novelty at the Meeting on the Ist Inst unless the judicious determination of the Directors and the proprietors, not to pay a Dividend until they could pay one, bona fide, may be deemed a Novelty.'[41]

Chapter 8
The first Metropolis Water Act

Following the end of competition in London's water supply
with the General Arrangement of 1817[1] among the water
companies, price was for a few years the main focus of controversy. Within a decade it had been superseded by rising discontent on other aspects – the intermittent supply system, and
especially the quality of the water supplied.

At the start of the century water from the Thames and from
the New River was of reasonably satisfactory quality, by the
standards of the time. By the 1820s, however, several factors
led to increasing sewage pollution in the Thames (and the Lee,
used as a main source by the East London Company and as a
subsidiary source by the New River Company). Growth in the
use of water-closets enormously increased the volume of
sewage so that cesspits were no longer adequate; sewers,
long used for surface water drainage only, were now common-
ly used to dispose of household waste water. This practice was
legalised in 1815. London's sewers generally led straight to
the nearest water course – minor rivers such as the Fleet, the
Lee or the Thames itself. The rapid growth of population and
the more plentiful supplies of water added to the pollution.

The problem was exacerbated by the tidal action of the
rivers which constantly mixed the pollution and prevented it
from being dispersed in the mud on the river bed or swiftly
carried out to sea, and also turned the mud-flats along the
Thames into noxious dunghills. In 1827 a celebrated pam-
phlet pointed out that the Grand Junction Company's inlet
from the Thames was almost opposite the Ranelagh sewer,
and maintained that the Thames water 'being charged with
the contents of more than 130 public common sewers, the
refuse of hospitals, slaughter-houses, colour, lead, gas and

Map, 1833. This map shows the companies' intakes at the height of the pollution. During the next five years several companies moved their intakes considerably further upstream.

soap-works, drug-mills and manufactories, and with all sorts of decomposed animal and vegetable substances, rendering the said water offensive and destructive to the health, ought no longer to be taken up by any of the companies from so foul a source'.[2]

The public agitation that followed led to the appointment of a Royal Commission, which in 1828 reported that the Thames and Lee should be abandoned as sources. Schemes were produced for substituting supplies from local rivers such as the Verulam and the Wandle, but these were condemned as impractical, probably rightly, by the companies' engineers. Instead of abandoning the tidal rivers the companies adopted various new measures to improve the quality of their supplies, including slow sand filtration (introduced by the Chelsea Company in 1829), 'subsiding reservoirs' in which the most obvious impurities were allowed to sink to the bottom, and moving the intakes upriver away from the most heavily polluted stretches. The Grand Junction Company moved its intake from Chelsea to Brentford in 1838, and the East London Company opened a new intake on the Lee at Lee Bridge in 1834 to replace the one at Old Ford. Minor agitations against the water companies persisted through the 1830s but had little effect; in 1840 a committee of the House of Lords endorsed the recommendations of the 1828 commission but took no action.

The two events which brought the affairs of the London water companies to a crisis were the advent of Edwin Chadwick and the Sanitary Association in the 1840s and the great cholera epidemic of 1848–49. Chadwick's *Report on the Sanitary Condition of the Labouring Population* (1842) roundly condemned the London water companies; they were said to be 'practically irresponsible and arbitrary, and unaccommodating towards individuals'.[3] His Utilitarian outlook was offended by the wastefulness of 'several expensive establishments and sets of officers, which appear to admit of consolidation'.[4] The largely Chadwickian *Health of Towns Reports* (1844–45) renewed the attack on the companies, particularly in the matter of the sources (the Thames in particular being condemned as too polluted to be used even after filtration), the intermittent system of supply, and the practice of providing communal standpipes to courts instead of individual supply pipes to houses.

Chadwick's schemes proposed that the companies should be bought out by the government (his opinion of the value of their works was such that only very small compensation was thought justified) and that the administration of the water supply and sewerage of the metropolis be placed in the hands of a small, government-appointed body. Water would be brought by aqueducts from gathering-grounds and springs to the north and south of London and distributed to all houses on a constant high-pressure system. The water discharged into the proposed drainage system would cleanse it automatically, and – best of all from the Utilitarian point of view – the resultant liquid sewage could be sold as manure, the profits paying for the administration of the whole scheme.

In the years after 1842 Chadwick made some progress towards achieving his goal. The setting up of the Metropolitan Commission of Sewers in 1847, with his the dominant voice on it, was an important victory for him, and the establishment of the General Board of Health in 1848 was a real triumph.

The outbreak of cholera in 1848 enabled Chadwick and his colleagues, such as the future Lord Shaftesbury, to embark on energetic programmes of sewer-flushing which would have been unacceptable in normal times, for the cholera had frightened all classes into accepting previously unthinkable measures of government interference. Again, while Chadwick himself did not accept Dr John Snow's theory that cholera was spread by polluted water supplies, preferring a 'miasmic' theory of bad air, Snow's ideas strengthened the case against the water companies and their use of the polluted Thames as a source of supply.

Chadwick launched his frontal attack on the companies with the *Report of the General Board of Health on Metropolitan Water Supply* (1850). It acknowledged that certain improvements had been made in recent years; five of the companies now filtered their supplies,[5] only three now drew their water from the most heavily polluted part of the Thames, and one (the Lambeth Company) was in the process of transferring its intake far up the river to Ditton instead of the present source at Battersea. The system of communal standpipes was being phased out. For example, only 731 of the 23,396 houses supplied by the Lambeth Company did not have direct supplies and this was typical. Most companies also now turned on the supplies every day (except Sundays) instead of on alternate days.

Nevertheless, the report was highly critical of the companies' conduct of their undertakings. Complaints about water quality were universal, despite filtration and settlement, the intermittent system resulted in further deterioration of quality while the water was stored in butts, and charges were excessive. Furthermore, the Thames water was found to be so hard as to be unsuitable for washing and for trade purposes, as well as polluted, and it was recommended that the Thames should be abandoned as a source. The report unsurprisingly recommended Chadwick's scheme of a government-appointed body to supervise London's water supply, drainage and sewerage as a single entity, and that water should be brought from the Farnham area in covered aqueducts and stored in covered reservoirs to replace existing sources of supply. It foresaw that 'an entirely new supply of water may be brought to our metropolis, pure, filtered and well aerated, and may be delivered into every house in the metropolis on a constant supply,

No. 1. is the Dolphin, or spot from which the Company derive their Supply.
2. is the mouth of the great Ranelagh Common Sewer.
3. is the Company's Steam-engine, which draws up the daily supply.
4. is Chelsea Hospital. At low water, the Dolphin is about three yards from the shore.

'The Dolphin'. The Grand Junction Company's intake in 1827, demonstrating the sources of pollution.

unlimited in quantity, for drinking, for culinary and other domestic purposes, for baths and for washing, at an average original rent-charge, inclusive of the expense of the tenant's supply pipe and tap, of 2d per week per tenement.'[6]

The water companies, then, found their monopolies under serious challenge. A whole series of Bills was introduced into Parliament with the object of providing alternative sources of supply. The Henley and London Waterworks Navigation Bill in 1849, the London (Watford) Spring Water Company Bill and the Metropolitan Waterworks (Henley-on-Thames and London Aqueduct) Bill in 1850 were defeated because the existing companies had interests active on their behalf in Parliament, but in 1851 Lord John Russell's government introduced a Metropolis Water Supply Bill.

This Bill, introduced by the Home Secretary, Sir George Grey, was largely designed by Sir William Clay, chairman of the Southwark and Vauxhall Water Works Company, and proposed the amalgamation of the water companies. It did not specify that new sources of water were to be used, but left this point open; it did include proposals for restrictions of dividends and special provisions for giving supplies to 'the inferior class of houses' and for cleaning and sanitary purposes. The new amalgamated company was to be placed under the control of a government department. Clay's intention was apparently to secure the companies' monopoly against such

**Opening of the Lambeth Company's Works, 1852. The
Lambeth Company was the first to move its intake
above the tideway. Its Seething Wells site, later known
as Surbiton Water Treatment Works, remained in use
for nearly 150 years.**

interlopers as the proposed Henley and Watford companies
and to forestall the public health enthusiasts, led by Chadwick
and in full cry after the companies, by a measure of voluntary
reform. All the other companies disagreed, however,
and fought the Bill, which was defeated. So was a simultane-
ous Bill moved by Francis Mowatt on behalf of the metropolitan vestries to place the water companies under vestry
control: this was opposed both by the companies and
Chadwick's supporters.

In February 1852 the struggle was renewed when the First
Commissioner of Works, Lord Seymour, who as President of
the General Board of Health had quarrelled with both
Chadwick and Shaftesbury, introduced a new Metropolis
Water Supply Bill into the Commons. In the meantime the
government had received an expert chemists' report which
discounted the Board of Health's prejudice against the
Thames and Lee as sources. Introducing the Bill, Seymour
said that water rates should be limited, and that the Board of
Health had recommended management by a commission
responsible to Parliament, although the government did not

agree. The Bill was intended to ensure the adequacy and purity of the sources of supply, 'but it was unnecessary there
should be any further interference, and if unnecessary it would
be unwise to interfere further';[7] Lord Seymour 'believed those
Companies would carry them out [i.e. new works] with more
efficiency and economy than any municipal corporation'.[8]
After the Bill had been introduced the Russell government fell,
but Lord John Manners, Seymour's successor in Lord Derby's
minority Conservative government, continued with the measure. It was considered in Committee together with a whole
batch of other legislation introduced by the various companies
to give them powers to execute new works. There was also a
Bill introduced by Francis Mowatt, intended to give the
vestries control over water supply (Metropolitan Water Supply
and Drainage Bill for vesting the Water supply and Drainage of
the Metropolis in Commissioners representing the Inhabitants
thereof) and another to set up the London (Watford) Spring
Water Company.

In drawing up the main Bill, Seymour had been advised by
Sir John Johnstone, chairman of the New River Company, and
the measure favoured the companies since they were to retain
their separate identities. The companies, however, considered
many of the proposals of the Bill objectionable, in particular
the clauses subjecting them to direct control by a Secretary of
State, the capping of water rates and the requirement to provide a constant supply throughout their statutory districts –
'although the Companies were willing to submit to any reasonable control there were certain clauses requiring great
modification'.[9] But in general the companies accepted the
clauses which obliged them to filter all river-derived water
(only the West Middlesex Company objecting) and to cover all
reservoirs for filtered water (the Lambeth Company being the
lone objector to this), nor did they oppose the requirement to
cease drawing water from the tidal Thames and Lee (except
the West Middlesex Company, which considered its Barnes
intake to be quite far enough upstream). Heated battles were
fought out in committee on the details of the clauses and the
principles of others, and mostly the companies' representatives carried their points.

When the Bill became law, the companies were made
responsible to the Board of Trade rather than directly to a
Secretary of State, and the clauses limiting charges were

removed. The clause requiring the supply of water to be constant – on which Derby had 'laid great stress' when defending
the Bill against Shaftesbury in the Lords – was so weakened in
committee as to be totally ineffective. In its final form, the
clause required a company to furnish a constant supply in any
main only if four-fifths of the owners or occupiers of the houses supplied from the main requested such a supply in writing,
and not even then if one-fifth of the houses did not have the
requisite apparatus in accordance with the company's regulations for receiving a constant supply. Not surprisingly, the New
River Company recorded that the new Act would require them
'in certain improbable circumstances to adopt the system of
Constant Supply'.[10]

The battle over the 1852 Metropolis Water Bill was a four-
cornered one. The protagonists were the government, clearly
anxious to allay public disquiet about water supplies but only
willing to assume the least possible responsibility itself, the
water companies, wishing to preserve their independence and
monopolies, the public health enthusiasts with their scheme
for centralised control of London's water supply and drainage,
and Mowatt with his proposal for municipal control. Mowatt
was the weakest of these. Although he enjoyed the powerful
support of *The Times*, the vestrymen he proposed to put in
control feared the resultant rate increases and gave him only
half-hearted support. The public health lobby was not represented before the committee, although Lord Ebrington spoke
at length on its behalf in the Commons and Shaftesbury spoke
in the Lords. Its influence had waned since the cholera panic
of 1848, and Chadwick and Shaftesbury had made many
enemies through their arrogance and disregard of vested interests. When the heavily-amended Bill finally reached the
Lords, Shaftesbury was ready to accept it as the best which
could be obtained, from his point of view. Derby pointed out to
him that to reject the Bill now would mean no improvement in
London's water supply for at least another year, until a fresh
bill could be prepared and introduced. The Metropolis Water
Act was therefore a compromise, and although it involved the
companies in great expense in constructing new works it did
leave them practically free from effective control for another
two decades.

The Act of 1852 was the first attempt to regulate London's
water supply, and is an interesting example of social legisla-

Hampton Water Treatment Works. Three companies co-operated to open a new intake and treatment works at Hampton, completed in 1856. The site is still London's largest water treatment works.

tion of the period. As it reached the statute book, its main provisions were as follows:

- It prohibited the drawing of water for domestic use from the tidal Thames or tributaries after 1855 (1856 for the Chelsea Company).
- It required all river-derived water for domestic use to be 'effectually filtered'.
- It required all reservoirs within five miles of St Paul's and containing filtered water to be covered.
- It required water for domestic use to be conveyed in pipes or covered aqueducts (rather than in open conduits like the New River) unless afterwards filtered.
- It empowered the Board of Trade to appoint an Inspector to investigate new sources of supply or complaints about water quality.
- It required the supply of water to be constant rather than intermittent (subject to certain conditions which were so stringent that this requirement was ineffectual).
- It placed an obligation on consumers to avoid wasting water, and empowered the companies to make regulations to prevent the waste or misuse of water.

- It empowered local parish authorities to compel owners of houses lacking water supplies to obtain them.

The most immediately obvious and expensive effect was that all the companies had at once to commence extensive new works to construct filter beds, cover reservoirs, install new pumping machinery and change their sources of supply, involving the laying of up to 13 miles of underground trunk mains in each case. In 1856 the General Board Health (from which all Chadwick's influence had now ben removed) reported that 'the new works have not in fact been limited to what a bare compliance with the provisions of the Act of 1852 would have fulfilled; measures have been adopted for the general improvement of the supplies which evinces a proper anxiety on the part of the Companies in the discharge of the duties of their position towards the public'.[11] Colonel Sir Francis Bolton, Water Examiner to the Local Government Board in the 1870s, considered that 'the Companies themselves had been aroused to a sense of their responsibilities'[12] by the agitation of 1850–52.

Few complaints about the quality of water supplies are recorded over the next decade, but the question of London's water came to the fore again as a result of the cholera epidemic of 1866, which affected mainly the area supplied by the East London Company. A select committee was set up in 1866 to examine, among other things, the working of the 1852 Act. The committee found that since 1852 the companies between them spent over £4 million on new works, and that 'both the quantity and quality of the water supplied from the Thames is so far satisfactory that there is no ground for disturbing the arrangements made under the Act of 1852'.[13] The cholera epidemic was thought to be due to contaminated water from the Lee seeping into the East London Company's covered reservoirs, but this was accepted as an accident and not a deliberate breach of the Act. The conclusion of the committee, however, was that 'the Act of 1852 has failed to secure for the inhabitants the advantage which they ought to have long since enjoyed of a well-regulated supply of water in their houses for domestic purposes',[14] because the companies had not yet introduced the constant supply system on any significant scale.

The Royal Commission on Water Supply, headed by the Duke of Richmond, reported in 1869. It found that while the sources of supply used by the companies were adequate, the purity of the water delivered to consumers ought to be improved by more efficient filtration. Like the select committee, the commission was very concerned by the lack of a constant supply, and this was its main reason for recommending the abolition of the companies and their replacement by a Chadwick-style public body. The commission believed that such a public body would be better able to carry out the large new works and enforce the stringent regulations which would be needed to enforce the new system.

A debate very like that of 1852 followed, with a similar result – Gladstone's government passed the Metropolis Water Act, 1871, leaving the companies in existence. Under the main provisions of this Act the companies were obliged to provide constant supplies under conditions much less stringent than those laid down under the 1852 Act. They were given powers to make regulations relating to consumers' water fittings and the associated powers of inspection, and a Water Examiner was to be appointed to watch over the purity of the water supplied. The companies then applied themselves, perforce, to extending the constant supply system, but as this entailed virtually replumbing every house in London and remodelling all the water works the process naturally took a long time. It was completed in 1899, three years before the Metropolis Water Act of 1902 which set up the Metropolitan Water Board to replace the companies.

Chapter 9
Competition yesterday and today

History, of course, never really repeats itself. Spotting parallels is entertaining but not necessarily instructive. Before looking at whether there are lessons to be learned in the present case, a summary of events during the past century may be helpful.

The Metropolis Water Act of 1902 seemed to have settled the disputes over London's water supply for good. The London County Council had stirred up agitation against the metropolitan water companies during the 1890s; two Royal Commissions followed, the second of which concluded that public ownership and indirect links with local government, but not outright control by the LCC, would be the best way forward. The government acted on this and created the Metropolitan Water Board, which acquired the operational assets of the eight companies in 1904. It was made up of representatives of the local authorities in its supply area, including the LCC and five county councils as well as numerous borough councils. It lasted for 70 years and earned a reputation for wise planning and prudent management. The former companies' works were integrated and extended, and plans for constructing ample storage reservoirs were carried out and further developed. Charges to customers were perceived as low,[1] and were based on property rental values in the same way as the general rates. Unobtrusive service was the keynote. The board fought off an attempt to incorporate it in the new Greater London Council in 1963,[2] and survived until the Heath government completely reconstituted the water industry of England and Wales.

The Water Act of 1973 abolished all the water boards,

municipal water departments, drainage departments, drainage boards and river conservancy boards in England and Wales. Their undertakings were consolidated into ten Regional Water Authorities, of which Thames Water, serving London and the Thames basin westwards to Gloucestershire, was the largest.[3] A National Water Council was established to co-ordinate the ten authorities. The MWB had been by far the largest of the water boards and formed the greater part of the Thames Water Authority. The new authority was constituted in the same way, with a large board made up of local authority representatives, and it continued its predecessor's unassuming style.

The next great change came in 1983. A new, dynamic Conservative government abolished the National Water Council and broke the historic links between water supply and local government. The large representative boards were scrapped and replaced by small, hand-picked boards in sympathy with the government's ideas. In Thames Water's case, the new chairman was Roy Watts, who was to be the leading exponent of water privatisation.

Watts raised the subject of privatisation almost immediately – no doubt with the full knowledge and support of the government. In 1986 the government issued a consultation paper proposing privatisation, along with a thorough review of water law. At that stage, the plans were deferred because of concern over the prospect of private companies, as managers of sewage treatment works the likeliest polluters of rivers, also being responsible as river authorities for pollution control. The solution, put forward in the 1989 Water Bill, was for the pollution control and river management functions to remain in the public sector, under a new National Rivers Authority, while the rest of each water authority was privatised.

So, in 1989, the ten regional water authorities passed their water supply and sewage disposal functions to ten new public limited companies. The largest and highest-profile was Thames Water Plc. Once again, water supply was in the hands of privately-owned monopolies. This time, though, there was a whole new regulatory framework to assure standards of service, control prices and maintain quality. In the ensuing years quality and service standards certainly rose,[4] but so did prices, in some cases staggeringly so. Over the country as a whole, water supply and sewerage charges rose by 41.6% in real terms between 1989 and 1998.[5]

The price increases were needed for several reasons. First, the water authorities had generally been less far-sighted than their predecessors such as the Metropolitan Water Board and investment in infrastructure replacement and extension had been at a low level. Much urgent modernisation was needed.[6] Second, various European Commission Directives mandated quality improvements, particularly in the quality of drinking water and the control of sewage sludge and effluent disposal. Third, public awareness of water-related matters, roused by the privatisation debate and the general growth of environmental concerns, was far greater than at any time in the previous century – another reason for expenditure on environment-related improvements.

Despite valiant attempts by the companies to publicise their achievements – which were very real – public perception saw them in general as greedy manipulators, extorting high prices for their own gain. The improvements to river water quality resulting from modernisation at sewage treatment works, for example, were invisible to most customers, while the customer service improvements were simply taken for granted. All the public noticed were the ever-larger bills dropping through their letter boxes each year. Well-publicised controversies about water metering, leakage and executive salaries made headlines. The effects of the drought in 1995 demonstrated that public sympathy with water companies had all but disappeared. During the country-wide drought of 1976, the public had put up more or less cheerfully with restrictions on hosepipe use, exhortations to re-use bathwater and prohibitions on car-washing. Nineteen years on the general attitude was that private companies which charged high prices should deliver the service no matter what. Yorkshire Water in particular was severely criticised.

During the 1997 General Election campaign, Labour exploited the unpopularity of water companies and found willing listeners; prices and leakage, especially, were constantly in the headlines. The new Labour government quickly announced action on both issues. A windfall tax on the supposed excess profits of the privatised companies accompanied strict controls on leakage. Both main political parties, meanwhile, had been looking at the prospects for competition in the water industry. The Conservative government had already opened up the way to some competition, but only for the largest customers, industrial firms who used over 250 mega-litres of water per year at a single site, and for developers building on green field sites. Although this limited competition was slow to develop, by 1999 a few large companies had switched suppliers and many more were looking at the possibilities.

Expectations were sharpened by the experience of the gas and electricity industries, which were being opened up in stages to full competition (using the concept of common carriage) several years ahead of the water industry. In fact, by 1999 water appeared to be the last bastion of monopoly. Inevitably, new firms appeared to take advantage of the opportunities. Their aim is brokerage deals, whereby they act as middlemen in order to force down the prices charged by the incumbent suppliers. The first such deal took place in 1999, transferring the supply to a paper mill from Welsh Water to new entrant Albion Water, but by mid-2000 the new firms had made little impression on the established companies. Indeed, those companies have started vigorous competition against each other – for example, in May 2000 Thames Water poached one of Mid-Kent Water's largest customers, the motor-racing circuit at Brands Hatch.

Competition is still difficult. There are regulatory hurdles to clear and the legislation is restrictive, but the impetus appears to be building. The common carriage concept is established in other utility industries and full freedom of choice for all customers is in prospect during the next few years, though it is likely to be a mixed blessing. The existing monopoly suppliers have legal obligations to serve all customers in their statutory areas, including many (especially in rural districts) who do not pay anything like enough to cover the cost of serving them. New entrants have no such obligations, and can cherry-pick profitable customers. Pressure to relate charges to the cost of serving individual customers is currently the lever used by new entrants; eventually it would have to be used defensively by incumbents. The effect would be a massive rebalancing of charges in favour of large industrial users and against rural householders – scarcely a popular change.

There are huge practical differences between nineteenth-century competition and that currently in prospect. Nobody now advocates different companies laying parallel water mains along the same streets and duplicating each other's infrastructures. The mechanisms now under consideration are brokerage, self-supply (large customers providing their own water sources from boreholes, and on-site sewage treatment facilities), inset appointments (one company serving customers within another company's geographical district),[7] and common carriage. These are more subtle than the Regency concept of direct competition, and also much harder for the ordinary customer to understand. But the essence of direct competition is there, and service standards are already so high that the only practical method is by price. It appears to me, after making every allowance for the different types of competition now being proposed, that the experiences of London's water suppliers between 1810 and 1817 do carry warnings for today.

Competition through price in Regency London ruined several companies (both old and new) and resulted in monopolies being established, with consequent price increases. Today there are regulatory controls aimed at avoiding monopolies – just as there were in 1817, when they proved to be ineffective. Unbridled competition today may well lead to a comparable period of chaos followed by de facto monopolies. The lessons I draw, then, are that government and regulators should proceed with extreme caution – and that would-be competitors should not expect to make easy fortunes. It may even be concluded that regulated monopolies, which were the norm between 1852 and the present, could be better providers of water and sewerage services than directly competitive suppliers. Time will tell.

Appendix
Historians' attitudes to the London water companies

In recent years, historians dealing with the controversies out-
lined above have tended to be very hostile to the water companies. A considerable degree of partisanship can be detected
in the many books published in the 1880s and 1890s on the
subject of London's water supply, but this is due to the London
County Council's various attempts at the time to gain control
of the water supply and some of the animus was against the
Council rather than the companies. R.A. Lewis and S.E. Finer,
however, in their first-class works on Edwin Chadwick, are
strongly opposed to the companies and are condemnatory of
the 1852 Act: Lewis considered that a great chance had been
missed by the Act's failure to place the companies under public control,[1] and Finer described the Act as scandalous.[2] This
attitude was followed by later historians such as Francis
Sheppard[3] and Royston Lambert, who regarded the Act as a
disgracefully cowardly measure which represented a surren-
der by the Government to the companies.[4] All these historians
appear to favour Chadwick's solution of a small, Government-
appointed body to control both the water supply and the
drainage of London. A.K. Mukhopadhyay, too, expressed hostility to the companies, evidently sympathising with reformers
struggling against the companies' vested interests and apparently starting from the assumption that 'public ownership' of
London's water supply is necessarily desirable.[5]

How fair is this prevailing attitude – an attitude which has
penetrated to many 'popular' works on London history and
general social history?

A study of the water companies' records, particularly their
minute books, clearly shows that throughout the period of the

greatest Public Health agitation they were actively engaged in improving their works despite the lack of any legal obligation to do so. During the 1840s the companies were using either filter beds or subsiding reservoirs to purify their water, several had moved their intakes upstream, at great expense, supplies were generally turned on six instead of three times a week, and by 1850 virtually all the old wooden pipes had been replaced by cast iron. New and more powerful pumping machinery was being installed to provide 'high service' (i.e. direct supplies to cisterns and taps at first-floor level .or above), and the 'high service charge' which was bitterly attacked by the companies' opponents was intended to defray the costs involved.

As the General Board of Health found in 1856, the companies were at the time expending larger sums on new works than would have been required to comply with the 1852 Act, and on water quality it was found in 1866 that 'the water supplied to the Metropolis contained not more than one-half of the organic matter which was present in the year 1851'.[6]

The Richmond Commission, which was certainly not biased in favour of the companies and recommended their abolition, found 'no evidence to lead us to believe that the water now supplied by the companies is not generally good and wholesome'[7] and 'We have reason to believe that the companies honestly do their best to supply the poor, and are inclined to be liberal in their arrangements for this purpose'.[8]

Both the 1866 Select Committee and the Richmond Commission fully realised the great difficulty involved in changing an undertaking designed for the intermittent supply system to enable the constant system to be introduced, and accepted that the companies were not deliberately obstructing the change. The Commission attributed the delay in introducing the new system to the reluctance of consumers and ratepayers to pay for changing plumbing installations within their houses. This was the principal reason for the Commission's recommendation that the companies should be abolished, for it was considered that only a public body could safely be entrusted with the 'inquisitorial' powers necessary to compel consumers to put and keep their plumbing in order.

There is plenty of evidence, then, that the companies were not nearly as bad as they have been portrayed. The readiness of most companies to sink large amounts of capital in improved works does not evidence indifference to the public good. Why, then, have so many historians condemned the companies and regretted their continued existence after 1852?

It is a point of interest that R.A. Lewis and S.E. Finer both based their admirable works largely on Edwin Chadwick's papers, and of course Chadwick was the arch-enemy of the water companies. Both Lewis and Finer fully recognised Chadwick's faults, but naturally they have tended to see things from Chadwick's point of view – and he always regarded any opposition as factious, unimaginative or sinister. The unfortunate sequel seems to have been that the general excellence of Lewis's and Finer's works has led to their views being accepted uncritically by later historians. It is significant that T. F. Reddaway, writing immediately before the publication of the two works on Chadwick, did not condemn the 1852 Act or the water companies; he considered that the Act represented a considerable advance and benefited the public as much as was then practicable.[9] The conclusive piece of evidence in favour of the companies in this period is that the 1866 Committee and the Richmond Commission found that in general they were doing their best to serve the public and were greatly improved since before the 1852 Act; there is no evidence that a publicly-controlled body would have done any better.

Abbreviations

1810 Minutes
> Evidence before the Committees of Both Houses of Parliament considering the West Middlesex WaterWorks Bill, 1810 (unpublished, printed for the West Middlesex Water Works Company, 1810)

1819 Minutes
> Minutes of evidence before the House of Lords committee on the West Middlesex and Grand Junction Water Works Bill, 1819 (unpublished)

1821 Minutes
> Parliamentary Papers: Minutes of Evidence taken before the Select Committee on the Supply of Water to the Metropolis, 1821

1821 Report
> Parliamentary Papers: Report of the Select Committee on the Supply of Water to the Metropolis, 1821

CWWC
> Minutes of the Courts of Directors of the Chelsea Water Works Company (unpublished)

ELWWC
> Minutes of the Meetings of the Directors of the East London Water Works Company (unpublished)

ELWWC – GA
> Minutes of the General Assemblies of the Proprietors of the East London Water Works Company (unpublished)

GJWWC
> Minutes of the Meetings of the Directors of the Grand Junction Water Works Company (unpublished)

GJWWC – GA
> Minutes of the General Assemblies of Proprietors of the Grand Junction Water Works Company (unpublished)

HLRO
    House of Lords Record Office
LBWW
    Minutes of the Meetings of the Committee of Managers of
    the London Bridge Water Works (unpublished)
LWWC
    Minutes of the Meetings of the Directors of the Lambeth
    Water Works Company (unpublished)
NRC
    Minutes of the Courts of Directors of the New River
    Company (unpublished)
PRO
    Public Record Office
SLWWC
    Minutes of the Meetings of the Directors of the South
    London Water Works Company (unpublished)
WMWWC
    Minutes of the Meetings of the Directors of the West
    Middlesex Water Works Company (unpublished)

Notes

Chapter 1
The possessors: the old water companies to 1805

1   Accounts of the history of the London Bridge Water Works are to be found in
     H.W. Dickinson, *Water Supply of Greater London* (Newcomen Society, London
     1954), and *The Water Supply of London*, published by the Metropolitan Water
     Board in 1961 and written by the Board's Archivist, Mr G. Berry.
2   1821 Report, Appendices B and L. This source gives figures of water supplied in
     hogsheads per year; I have converted these into gallons per day, taking one
     hogshead as $52^{1}/_{2}$ imperial gallons.
3   Dickinson, op. Cit, p 25.
4.   1821 Report, Appendix B
5   Dickinson, op cit, 35–41; Berry, op cit, 7–8; J. Jeffery, *The Statutory Water
     Companies.*(London 1981), pp 9–10.
6   1821 Report, Appendix B.
7   Berry, op cit, 8; R.E. Morris, *History of the New River* (Metropolitan Water
     Board, London 1934).
8   1821 Report, Appendices C and L.
9   WMWWC, 9 August 1815: report of the Committee negotiating with the New
     River Company.
10   1821 Report, Appendix C.
11   Dickinson, op cit, pp 55–58; Berry, op cit, 13; W. Matthews, *Hydraulia, An
     Historical and Descriptive Account of the Water Works of London* (London
     1835), pp 80–84.
12   1821 Report, Appendix L.
13   Ibid. Appendix D.
14   Matthews, op cit, p 84.
15   1810 Minutes.
16   Berry, op. Cit. 12: Dickinson, op cit, pp 48–49.
17   1821 Report, Appendix L.
18   David Murray, *The York Buildings Company* (Glasgow 1883).
19   1821 Report, Appendix E.
20   Berry, op cit, p 12.
21   Berry, op cit, 16: Dickinson, op cit, pp 49-51.
22   ELWWC, 17 March 1808.
23   Ibid.
24   1821 Report, Appendix L.
25   The Parliamentary Select Committee investigating the water companies in
     1821 found that 'The (New River) company's books ... do not furnish any
     means for distinguishing the amount received for water supplied for domestic

purposes, and for water used for the purposes of trade or manufacture.' (1821 Report, Appendix C).

26 1821 Report, Appendix L.
27 Berry, op cit, 24: Dickinson, op cit, pp 30-31.
28 R. Sisley, *The London Water Supply* (London 1899), p 22.
29 Berry, op cit, p 23.
30 Dickinson, op cit, 118; Matthews, op cit, pp 66–67.
31 Dickinson, op cit, 57: Morris, op cit, p 9.
32 1821 Minutes: evidence of William Chadwell Mylne.
33 Berry, op cit, p 25.
34 1810 Minutes: evidence of John Freeman, and questions put by Wetherell, Counsel for the West Middlesex Water Works Company.
35 ELWWC, 14 November 1810.
36 1821 Minutes: evidence of William Chadwell Mylne.
37 Berry, op cit, p 27: Dickinson, op cit, pp 49 and 63–64.
38 Berry, op cit, p 27.
39 Dickinson, op cit, pp 49–51.
40 Ibid,p 65.
41 Ibid, pp 68–70.
42 Dickinson, op cit, p 118.
43 Berry, op cit, p 25: Dickinson, op cit, p 118: 1810 Minutes, evidence of Thomas Simpson.
44 Berry, op cit, 25: Dickinson, op cit, p 118.
45 Dickinson, op cit, p 118.
46 1810 Minutes.
47 Matthews, op cit, p 71.
48 1810 Minutes, evidence of William Yambold.
49 1810 Minutes.
50 R. Dodd, *Observations on Water: With a Recommendation of a more Convenient and Extensive Supply of Thames Water, to the Metropolis, and its Vicinity, as the best Means To counteract Pestilence or Pernicious Vapours* (London 1805), p 75.
51 1810 Minutes.
52 D. Marshall, *Industrial England, 1776–1851* (London 1973), pp 29–30.
53 F. Sheppard, *London 1808–1870: The Infernal Wen* (Secker and Warburg, London 1971), p 25.
54 1821 Report, Appendix C.
55 L. Lambton, *Temples of Convenience* (London 1978), pp 5–9.
56 ELWWC, 12 July 1809. The Company charged two guineas extra for a fixed bath, as against 5s. for a two-stall stable and half a guinea for a water closet.1 1821 Report, Appendix C.
57 F. Place, Additional MSS 27828, folio 120 ff, quoted in M.D. George, *London Life In the Eighteenth Century* (Kegan Paul, London 1925), Peregrine edition (1966), pp 71–72.
58 F. Place, *Principles of Population* (1822), quoted in George, op cit, p 72.
59 Ralph, *Critical Review* (1783), quoted in George, op cit, pp 110–111.
60 1810 Minutes, evidence of John Johnson.
61 Dickinson, op cit, p 76: Sisley, op cit, p 23.

Chapter 2
The newcomers: the establishment of the South London, West Middlesex and East London Water Works Companies, 1805–1810

1 1 W. Matthews, *Hydraulia, An Historical and Descriptive Account of the Water Works of London* (London 1835), p 119.
2 Ibid, p 121.
3 Ibid, p 123.
4 J.G. James, 'Ralph Dodd, The Very Ingenious Schemer', in *Transactions of the Newcomen Society*, vol 47 (1974–6), pp 161–178.
5 R. Dodd, *Observations on Water: With a Recommendation of a more Convenient and Extensive Supply of Thames Water, to the Metropolis, and its Vicinity, as the best Means to counteract Pestilence or Pernicious Vapours* (London 1805).
6 Ibid. Appendix 2.
7 Ibid.
8 SLWW.
9 Ibid, 24 August 1805.
10 Ibid, 12 August 1805.
11 Ibid, 13 August 1807.
12 Ibid, 6 June 1808 and 5 June 1809.
13 Ibid, 4 June 1810.
14 SLWWC, 13 August 1807: also LWWC, 18 August 1807.
15 LWWC, 8 December 1807.
16 Ibid, 5 April 1808.
17 Ibid, 25 February, 4 April and 25 April 1810.
18 There was an outbreak of fierce competition among the water companies south of the Thames between 1839 and 1842.
19 HLRO, Deposited Plan, H.L., 1806, Kensington Waterworks Bill.
20 Estimate deposited with plan, HLRO.
21 William Nicholson (1753–1815) had published many scientific books and worked as a patent agent before turning his talents to water works. He was much in demand as a 'scientific umpire'. See entry in *Dictionary of National Biography*.
22 WMWWC, 17 September to 13 November 1806. The account of this incident given by M.K. Knight to the 1821 Parliamentary Select Committee and followed by Matthews in *Hydraulia* (1835) is incorrect. Knight stated that Dodd originally proposed Hammersmith as the site for the works, then changed his mind and wanted to build them at Pooles Creek.
23 WMWWC: Directors' Report to General Assembly, 3 November 1807.
24 WMWWC, 29 June 1807.
25 Ibid, 24 December 1807
26 Ibid, 29 March 1808.
27 Ibid, 3 November 1807. Ralph Walker was already an experienced engineer, having been employed with John Rennie and others as an arbitrator for the London Dock Company in 1800, and involved with the construction of the London, East India and West India Docks. He was Engineer at various times to the East London, West Middlesex and Portsmouth and Farlington Water Works.
28 WMWWC, 9 February 1808.
29 1821 Report, p 3.
30 WMWWC, 3 May 1808.
31 Ibid, 24 December 1807 and 3 March 1808.

32 WMWWC, 21 and 23 November 1809.
33 Ibid, 3 May 1808.
34 Ibid, 14 February 1809.
35 Ibid, 10 August 1809.
36 Ibid, 13 and 17 July 1809.
37 WMWWC, 3 November 1809.
38 Ibid, 7 November 1809.
39 Ibid, 19 April 1810.
40 Ibid, 28 November 1809.
41 1810 Minutes.
42 WMWWC, 21 May 1810.
43 Ibid, 7 November 1809.
44 Dodd, op cit, Appendix 2. The reference to filtering is interesting, but this proposal was not adopted: no London water company filtered its water before 1829, and the East London Company did not do so until compelled by statute after 1852. See M.N. Baker, *The Quest For Pure Water* (New York 1948), pp 89–90.
45 Dodd, op cit, Appendix 2.
46 HLRO, Deposited Plan, H.L. 1807, East London Waterworks Bill.
47   HLRO, Committee Book, H.L., 31 July 1807.
48 ELWWC, 16 December 1807 and 25 January 1808.
49 ELWWC, 25 August 1807.
50 Ibid, 14 October 1807.
51 Ibid, 17 March 1808.
52 Ibid, 2 April 1808.
53   Ibid, 29 June 1808.
54 Ibid, 27 July and 10 August 1808.
55 Ibid, 1 April 1809.
56 ELWWC, various dates, 10 August 1808 to 30 August 1809.
57 Ibid, 21 and 28 June 1809.
58 Ibid, 5 October 1809.
59 ELWW, various dates, 13 September to 23 October 1809: also *The Times*, 28 October 1809, which carried a full report of the proceedings. Princess Amelia died in the following year, at the age of 27.

Chapter 3
Competition 1810–1815

1   WMWWC, 7 November 1809.
2   Ibid, 7 May 1811.
3   Ibid, 2 October 1811.
4   WMWWC, 20 March 1812: *The Times*, 18 November 1812.
5   ELWWC, 26 March, 4 April and 2 May 1810.
6   ELWWC, 29 October 1812.
7   GJWWC, 5 July 1811.
8   Ibid.
9   Ibid, 12 July 1811.
10 Ibid, 25 July 1811.
11 Ibid, 16 September 1811.
12 Ibid, 3 and 10 July 1812.
13 GJWWC, 5 March 1813.
14 GJWWC – GA, 3 December 1812.
15 Ibid, 7 December 1815.

16 1821 Minutes: evidence of James Dupin
17 Ibid.
18 ELWWC, 14 June 1809.
19 Ibid, 21 June 1809.
20 NRC, 12 July 1810.
21 Ibid, 21 February 1811.
22 Ibid, 22 February 1811.
23 NRC, 13 February 1812.
24 Ibid, 30 April 1812.
25 Ibid, 16 July 1812.
26 Ibid, 27 May 1813 and 20 April 1815.
27 Ibid, 6 May 1813.
28 Ibid, 3 September 1812.
29 Ibid, 26 March 1812.
30 Ibid, 10 September 1812.
31 NRC, 21 January 1813.
32 Ibid, 11 February 1813.
33 Ibid, 25 February 1813.
34 WMWWC: Directors' Report to General Assembly, 2 November 1813.
35 NRC, 19 December 1811.
36 Ibid, 27 August 1812.
37 NRC, 16 February 1817.
38 Ibid, 28 July 1814.
39 Ibid, 6 May 1813.
40 Letter from M.K. Knight, West Middlesex Company Secretary, to New River
     Company, 28 April 1813.
41 Letter from M.K. Knight to New River Company, 9 December 1814.
42 Letters from M.K. Knight to New River Company, 12, 18 and 28 January 1815.
43 *Morning Post*, 21 and 22 December 1814.
44 GJWWC–GA, 1 June 1815.
45 1821 Report, Appendices C and L.
46 Letter to *The New Times*, 14 May 1819.
47 LBWW, 3 January 1812.
48 Ibid, 6 November 1812.
49 Ibid, 15 November 1816.
50 Ibid, 18 September and 24 January 1812.
51 These figures are taken from the Company's share transfer certificates.
52 1821 Minutes: evidence of Joseph Steevens.
53 ELWWC, 17 October 1813.
54 ELWWC-GA, 3 April 1812.
55 Now Regents Park.
56 WMWWC, 20 March 1812.
57 WMWWC, 30 September 1812, 27 January and 2 November 1813.
58 Ibid, 2 May and 16 August 1815.
59 Ibid, 5 September 1815.
60 GJWWC, 16 and 23 October 1812.
61 GJWWC-GA, 2 December 1813.
62 Ibid, 2 June and 1 December 1814.
63 GJWWC-GA, 1 June 1815, 6 June 1816 and 5 June 1817.
64 Ibid, 4 December 1817.
65 Ibid, 6 June 1816.

Chapter 4
Agreement 1815–1818
1   NRC, 6 May 1813
2   Ibid, 6 and 20 May 1813
3   Ibid, 9 November 1815.
4   NRC, 28 September 1815
5   ELWWC-GA, 1 February and 4 April 1816.
6   Ibid, 6 July 1817.
7   Ibid, 1 October 1818.
8   WMWWC, 9 August 1815.
9   Ibid, 5 September 1815.
10 WMWWC, 7 November 1815.
11 Letter from M.K. Knight to William Ford, 19 October 1815.
12 NRC, 8 February 1816.
13 WMWWC, 20 March and 7 May 1816.
14 GJWWC - GA, 6 June 1816.
15 WMWWC, 29 May 1816.
16 Ibid, 14 August 1816.
17 Ibid, 1 May 1818; the negotiating Committee's report is dated January 1817 but was not entered in the Minute s until over a year later.
18 1821 Minutes: evidence of R. Till.
19 Letter from J. Bailey (of the West Middlesex Company) to Messrs. Rose, Booker and Webb, Scavengers of Marylebone, 9 November 1812.
20 NRC, 20 March 1816.
21 LBWW, 15 November 1816.
22 Ibid, 14 November 1817.
23 Ibid.
24 NRC, 21 May 1816.
25 Ibid, 10 March 1818.
26 David Murray, *The York Buildings Company* (Glasgow 1883), p 111.
27 *The Water Supply of London* (Metropolitan Water Board, 1961), p 12.
28 CWWC, 30 May 1816.
29 Ibid, 27 June 1816.
30 Ibid, 11 July 1816.
31 Ibid, 7 August 1816.
32 Ibid, 17 March 1817.
33 Ibid.
34 Ibid.
35 Ibid, 10 July 1817.
36 WMWWC, 5 May 1818.
37 CWWC, 10 July 1817.
38 WMWWC, 5 May 1818.
39 CWWC, 16 October 1817.
40 Ibid, 26 October 1820 and 5 July 1821.
41 WMWWC, 6 May 1817.

Chapter 5
The question of charges 1818–1821
1   F.H.W. Sheppard, *Local Government in St Marylebone 1688–1835* (London 1958), p 128.
2   1819 Minutes (appended list).
3   R. Price-Williams, 'The Population of London 1801-1881', in *Journal of the*

Statistical Society, vol. 48 (1885).

4   Sheppard, op cit, pp 131–163.
5   According to Sheppard, op cit, 194, the Vestry's Surveyor was in 1812
    employing 81 men simply to repair the paving torn up by the water companies.
    The companies did, however, pay for the expense involved.
6   1821 Minutes: evidence of John Thomas Hope.
7   Ibid: evidence of John Richardson
8   1821 Report, Appendix A: also WMWWC, 23 January 1818.
9   1821 Report, Appendix A: also WMWWC, 6 February 1818.
10 WMWWC, 6 and 18 February 1818
11 Ibid, 24 February 1818.
12 1821 Report, Appendix A.
13 WMWWC, 24 February 1818.
14 1821 Report, Appendix A: also WMWWC, 26 February 1818.
15 1821 Report, Appendix A: also WMWWC, 4 and 6 March 1818.
16 1821 Report, Appendix A: also letter from West Middlesex Company to
    Marylebone Select Vestry, 28 March 1818.
17 1821 Report, Appendix A: also GJWWC–GA, 4 June 1818.
18 WMWWC, 8 May 1818.
19 WMWWC, 3 November 1818.
20 GJWWC–GA, 3 December 1818.
21 1821 Minutes, evidence of W. Coe and M.K. Knight.
22 Ibid, evidence of Robert Kerrison.
23 Ibid, evidence of William Harris.
24 1819 Minutes: speech of Jackson.
25 1819 Minutes: evidence of W. Coe and M.K. Knight.
26 1819 Minutes: evidence of Peter Potter.
27 Ibid: evidence of Pollock.
28 Sheppard, op cit, p 197.
29 Ibid, 198: also GJWWC–GA, 1 July 1819.
30 1821 Minutes: evidence of M.K. Knight.
31 Ibid.
32 GJWWC–GA, 1 June 1820.
33 Ibid.
34 Ibid.
35 GJWW–GA, 7 December 1820.
36 ELWWC–GA, 12 February 1819.
37 1821 Minutes: evidence of J.B. Sharpe and J. Davies.
38 *The Times*, 31 October 1818.
39 ELWWC–GA, 12 February 1819.
40 ELWWC–GA, 1 April 1819.
41 GJWWC–GA, 7 June 1821: also *The Times*, 7 February 1821.

Chapter 6
The Parliamentary Select Committee of 1821
1   This chapter is based almost entirely on the 1821 Minutes and Report. I have
    not given detailed page-references throughout the chapter.
2   *The Times*, 7 February 1821.
3   *The Times*, 15 June 1821

Chapter 7
Fraud and investment: the men behind the companies

1   R. Dodd, *Observations on Water* (London 1805).
2   The younger Dodd was generally known as Robert, signing himself B.R., R. and Robert Dodd on different occasions. This has led to confusion of him with his father: for instance H.W. Dickinson, in *The Water Supply of Greater London* (London 1954) misnames Ralph as Robert.
3   *The Times*, 16 August 1810.
4   *The Times*, 31 May 1808. The records of the case held in the British Museum were destroyed in an air-raid in 1940.
5   ELWWC, 1 and 15 September 1807. In the event, the advertisement appeared without the reference to Dodd.
6   ELWWC, 14 October 1807.
7   C. Hadfield, *British Canals* (6th Edn, London 1979), p 157.
8   J.G. James, 'Ralph Dodd, the Very Ingenious Schemer', in *Transactions of the Newcomen Society*, Vol. 47 (1974–6), 161–178; also *Annual Biography and Obituary* (London 1823).
9   Quoted in James, loc cit, p 161.
10 Ibid.
11 G. Rudé *Hanoverian London 1714–1808* (London 1971), p 249.
12 PRO, Chancery Records, Division II, Winter, Johnson and Turton; Bundle 636 (East London Water Works Company-v-Hubbard); Bundle 645 (East London Water Works Company-v-Mainwaring).
13 ELWWC, 18 August 1807.
14 As note 12; pleading by Counsel for the plaintiffs.
15 Ibid: also ELWWC–GA, 7 January 1808.
16 Ibid.
17 ELWWC-GA, 8 April 1808.
18 East London Water Works Company-v-Mainwaring, loc cit.
19   ELWWC-GA, 6 October 1808.
20 `ELWWC-GA, 17 November 1808.
21 East London Water Works Company-v-Hubbard and Mainwaring, loc cit; also ELWWC-GA, 6 April 1809.
22 GJWWC-GA, 3 December 1812.
23 East London Water Works Company-v-Mainwaring, loc cit.
24 Ibid.
25 See Chapter 2, above.
26 WMWWC, 6 November 1810.
27   WMWWC, 3, 17 and 23 January 1811.
28 ELWWC-GA, 5 April 1810; ELWWC, 11 April 1810.
29 ELWWC-GA, 4 February 1812.
30 1821 Minutes: evidence of James Dupin.
31 *The Times*, 16 August 1813.
32 1819 Minutes.
33 The Mississippi Scheme was the French equivalent of the South Sea Bubble: fantastic increases in share prices were followed by a catastrophic fall. Law had to flee the country after the collapse.
34 1821 Minutes: evidence of James Weale.
35   1821 Minutes: evidence of M.K. Knight.
36 These figures are taken from the incomplete surviving share transfer certificates of the West Middlesex Company.
37   M.K. Knight to William Ford, 28 August 1815.

38 Ibid.
39 M.K. Knight to William Ford, 20 September 1815.
40 M.K. Knight to William Ford, 19 October 1815.
41 M.K. Knight to John Daniel Hose, 9 November 1814.

Chapter 8
The first Metropolis Water Act
1   There was a further outbreak of competition among the South London companies in 1839–42, resulting in the amalgamation of the Southwark and Vauxhall Companies and lasting ill-feeling towards the Lambeth Company.
2   Quoted in Shadwell, A, *The London Water Supply*, (Longman, London 1899).
3   'The Sanitary Condition of the Labouring Population'. Report by Edwin Chadwick, published by the *Poor Law Commissioners, 1842*. (Edinburgh University Press edition, 1965), pp 144–45
4   Ibid, p 144
5   'Report of the General Board of Health on Metropolitan Water Supply', London 1850, Appendix.
6   Ibid, p 116.
7   Hansard, vol 119, pp 216–7.
8   Ibid, pp 219–20.
9   NRC, 18 March 1852.
10 Ibid, 1 July 1852
11 Scratchley, P.A. *London Water Supply, incorporating Bolton's London Water Supply*, (Wm Clowes and Sons, 1888), p 18.
12 Ibid, p 19.
13 'Report from the Select Committee on East London Water Bills and the Operation of the Metropolis Water Act, 1852', Parliamentary Papers, 1867, para 28.
14 Ibid, para 69.

Chapter 9
Competition yesterday and today
1   Although they were not as low as nostalgic customers of today believe – the MWB's average household bill in 1945/46 was £4.19s.11d, compared with its successor's average for water supply of £99 in 1998/99. After adjusting for inflation (a factor of about 20), we can see that the real charge is about the same.
2   For the 1963 controversy, see A K Mukhopadhyay, 'The Politics of London Water' in *The London Journal*, 1975.
3   A Labour government would no doubt have made a clean sweep. The Conservative government of 1973 left the 30-odd statutory water companies, some of them supplying water to London suburbs, untouched. This led to the odd situation whereby most of the new water authorities provided sewerage services to all of their areas but water supply to only part – causing lasting confusion to customers.
4   The annual Levels of Service Reports issued by the Office of Water Services clearly show marked improvements against all service measures – generally disregarded, alas, by heedless customers.
5   Figures given in Water and Sewerage Bills 1998–1999, issued by the Office of Water Services.
6   A good example is the Tunnel Ring Main around London. The Metropolitan

Water Board perceived the need and started planning as early as the 1950s; construction started in the early 1970s but was halted in 1975 leaving the stand-alone Southern Tunnel Main. Work restarted in 1986, and was accelerated by the new privatised company after 1989. The main was completed, as the Thames Water Ring Main, in 1994.

7   An example is that of Tidworth, a small town in Wiltshire consisting mainly of Ministry of Defence property and situated in Wessex Water's area. In 1998 Thames Water obtained an inset appointment to manage the town's (self-contained) water supply and sewerage systems.

Appendix
Historians' attitudes to the London water companies

1   Lewis, R. A., *Edwin Chadwick and the Public Health Movement 1832–1854*, (Longman, London 1952), p 328.
2   Finer, S. E., *The Life and Times of Sir Edwin Chadwick*, (Methuen, London 1951), p 423.
3   Sheppard, F., *London 1808–1870: The Infernal Wen*, (Secker & Warburg London 1971), pp 275, 294.
4   Lambert, R., *Sir John Simon, 1816–1904, and English Social Administration*, (MacGibbon & Kee, London 1963), pp 177, 178, 269.
5   Mukhopadhyay, A.K., 'The Politics of London Water', *London Journal*, 1975.
6   'Report from the Select Committee on East London Water Bills and the Operation of the Metropolis Water Act 1852', 1867, para 23.
7   'Report of the Royal Commission on Water Supply' 1869, para 214.
8   Ibid, para 244.
9   Reddaway, T. F., *London in the Nineteenth Century: the Fight for a Water Supply*, (London 1950), p 129.
10 Mukhopadhyay, op cit, pp 220–222.

Bibliography and sources

Primary sources in manuscript

This book is based principally on the Minute books of the various water companies, which were then held by the Thames Water Authority at New River Head. All are unpublished and in manuscript, and are listed below. The Thames Water Authority's archives were presented in 1991 by its successor to the Greater London Record Office (now the London Metropolitan Archive).

Minutes of the Meetings of the Directors of the South London Water Works Company 1805–1821.

Minutes of the Meetings of the Directors of the West Middlesex Water Works Company 1806–1821.

Minutes of the Meetings of the Directors of the East London Water Works Company 1807–1821.

Minutes of the General Assemblies of the Proprietors of the East London Water Works Company 1807–1821.

Minutes of the Meetings of the Directors of the Grand Junction Water Works Company, 1811–1821.

Minutes of the General Assemblies of the Proprietors of the Grand Junction Water Works Company 1811–1821.

Minutes of the Courts of Directors of the Chelsea Water Works Company 1805–1821.

Minutes of the Courts of Directors of the New River Company 1805–1821.

Minutes of the Meetings of the Directors of the Lambeth Water Works Company 1805–1821.

Minutes of the Meetings of the Directors of the Kent Water Works Company 1809–1810.

Minutes of the Meetings of the Committee of Managers of the London Bridge Water Works Company 1805–1821.

The Thames Water Authority also held the Letter Books, Dividend Books and some of the share transfer certificates of the West Middlesex Water Works Company for this period, and two books of press cuttings apparently compiled by that Company.

Another manuscript source held by the Thames Water Authority was: *Minutes of Evidence before the Lords Committee considering the West Middlesex and Grand Junction Water Works Bill 1819.* This does not appear to have been printed, presumably because the Bill failed.

Other manuscript sources include:

House of Lords Committee Books 51, 52 and 53 (1806–7), containing evidence concerning the original plans for the West Middlesex and East London water works, held in the House of Lords.

Pleadings in the case of the Company of Proprietors of the East London Water Works vs George Boulton Mainwaring and others (1809), held in the Chancery Records of the Public Record Office.

Printed primary sources

Parliamentary Papers: *Report of* and *Minutes of Evidence taken before the Parliamentary Select Committee on the Supply of Water to the Metropolis* 1821.

Minutes of Evidence before Committees of Both Houses of Parliament on the West Middlesex Water Works Bill 1810 (not included in Parliamentary Papers, but printed for the Company; the Thames Water Authority and Institution of Civil Engineers had copies).

Ralph Dodd, *Observation on Water, with a Recommendation of a more Convenient and Extensive Supply of Thames Water, to the Metropolis, and its Vicinity, As the best Means to Counteract Pestilence or Pernicious Vapours,* London 1805.

The Times, 1805–1821.

Entries on John Rennie (1822) and Ralph Dodd (1823) in *Annual Biography* and *Obituary.*

Secondary sources

W. Matthews, *Hydraulia; An Historical and Descriptive Account of the Water Works of London, &c.,* London 1835
Matthews' work is an ambitious attempt to describe the water works of cities ranging from ancient Athens and Alexandria to modern Paris and Constantinople, together with a history of the development of London's water supply. He gives a fairly full account of the period 1805–21 and strongly takes the side of the companies against their critics, although giving no names of individuals involved in the controversy of 1818–21.

David Murray, *York Buildings Company*, Glasgow 1883.
Murray deals mainly with the activities of the York Buildings Company in buying and selling Scottish property in the eighteenth century, touching only briefly on its London water works.

F. Bolton, *London Water Supply*, revised by P.A. Scratchley, London 1888.
Colonel Sir Francis Bolton was the first Water Examiner appointed under the Metropolis Water Act, 1871. His book is mainly a description of the water companies' systems in the 1870s and 1880s; although a historical sketch is included it barely mentions the competition period.

H.L. Cripps, *The Position of the London Water Companies*, London 1892.
Cripps was a lawyer employed by the London County Council to assess the legal position of the London water companies, with a view to the Council's acquiring their undertakings. His published report contains little of relevance to the early part of the century.

R. Sisley, *The London Water Supply*, London 1899.
Sisley outlines the development of the London water companies in the light of the current controversy between them and the London County Council. He gives some useful details concerning the competition period, including an account of the Pocock's Well incident.

A. Shadwell, *London Water Supply*, London 1899.
Shadwell defends the companies against contemporary criti-

cism. He writes patronisingly of the early nineteenth-century companies that they did their best, and that their level of service was acceptable to a public which had never known anything better. His main point is to show that the companies had developed a satisfactory system without control by local government.

H.C. Richards and W.H.C. Payne, *London Water Supply*, London 1899.
Richards was a Member of Parliament and Payne a London County Councillor. Their book is heavily critical of the companies and in favour of their abolition and replacement by LCC control. Of its 294 pages, only the first fourteen are concerned with the period up to 1821. The main part of the work is concerned with the law as it stood in the 1890s.
    After the controversies of the 1890s had been settled by the establishment of the Metropolitan Water Board in 1903, no history of London's water supply was published for half a century.

R.E. Morris, *History of the New River*, Metropolitan Water Board, 1934.
Morris gives an anecdotal history of the New River Company, with useful descriptions of its works at various times. As an engineer, his main interest in the early nineteenth century is in the work of William Chadwell Mylne, and he does not mention the competition.

H.W . Dickinson, *Water Supply of Greater London*, London 1954 (originally published in *The Engineer* 1948).
Dickinson gives a fairly full history of the development of London's water supply. His main interest is in the pumping machinery used, however, and he gives only brief mentions to the competition period. He is generally hostile to the nineteenth-century water companies, and refers to the 1821 Select Committee as having 'whitewashed' them.

T.F. Reddaway, 'London In the Nineteenth Century, The Fight For A Water Supply' in *The Nineteenth Century and After*, London 1952.
Reddaway's article is concerned mainly with the mid-century controversies about water quality, and the growth of

Government control over the water companies. He recognises the significance of the competition episode in its effect on the relationship between companies and consumers, but does not give a detailed account of events in the period.

F.H.W. Sheppard, *Local Government in St Marylebone 1688–1835*, London 1958.
Sheppard's entertaining book gives a good account of the competition from the point of view of the Marylebone Select Vestry.

The Water Supply of London, Metropolitan Water Board, 1961 (unattributed, but written by G.C. Berry).
Berry was the Metropolitan Water Board's archivist, and his book contains a highly condensed and factual historical account of London's water supply. It gives many facts concerning the establishment of the new companies in 1805-1811, but only a brief mention of the competition and the 1821 Select Committee.

F.H.W. Sheppard, *London 1808–1870: The Infernal Wen*, London 1971.
Sheppard gives a short account of the competition period as an introduction to his fuller treatment of the later public health controversy. He largely follows Reddaway.

J. Jeffery, *The Statutory Water Companies, Their History and Development*, London 1981.
Jeffery's purpose is to give the histories of those water companies which are still in existence, but he does describe the development of the London companies. He briefly describes the competition and the findings of the 1821 Select Committee.

Index